YOU, ME and
ADHD Doing it Differently

The NON-ADHD Partners Guide To Finding Peace

By K. Fritts

ISBN 979-8-98874-290-6

DEDICATION

In honor of all those who have been a part of this rollercoaster, I have called life. Each person has added value and insight. Thank you.

A shout out to my boys!!! The laughter, tears and memories we share are my most cherished gifts. Thank you for giving me the space to grow up with you, learn with and from you, and for being my reason for living. I couldn't be more proud or more grateful. I am blessed to be your mom.

TABLE OF CONTENTS

☞ FOREWORD

Like many books, this too has a story born from necessity. Years of searching, studying, and muddling my way through a relationship affected by ADHD, I found little to no support for the Partner. I saw the need, the necessity, to help the partners of those with ADHD.

Similar to many of your stories, ours began with an addiction like chemistry. We met on New Year's Eve 2014 followed by a whirlwind of texts and phone calls throughout the day and night, hours of conversation, dinners out, dancing, fun filled weekends and sex....Oh the sex! By Valentine's weekend, we were both hooked.
He was vibrant, entertaining, and had a boyish charm that seemed sweet and innocent. Our relationship felt like an addiction. Little did I know.

In December of the same year, I had moved myself and my 3 boys into his home. That is when the HYPERFOCUS stopped. Panic at the disco!

We had tons of fun. Adventures abound with an ADHD partner. We were always on the go, camping, traveling and attending sporting events.

Random spontaneous events were often thrown in too. By our 1-year anniversary, we were living as strangers, going through the motions, and the tension was palpable.

At what point my partner had disclosed that he had been diagnosed with ADHD,I don't quite recall, but it seemed irrelevant during all the other crap going on in our life. It wasn't!

Having zero experience with ADHD, I didn't realize what an effect it was having and chalked all our issues up to a dysfunctional relationship.

I hit a point in our relationship that I was just done with it all, but I'm stubborn, so before throwing in the towel, I sought more answers and stumbled upon a book called The ADHD Effect On Marriage by Melissa Orlov. I saw my pain in the pages and for the first time; I saw his pain too. This inspired me to learn more.

I found very little support for the Non-ADHD partner. No inspiring words on how to stay in an ADHD affected relationship. No course on how to love ourselves through lonely times. And no path to finding some sense of sanity when we were the only ones working on solutions.

I found books, programs, articles, podcasts or the like, on how to help the ADHD partner. How we can make THEIR life better. All contain great ideas and certainly I recommend delving into those options for help. However, the **partners** of those with ADHD seem to get fluffed over, pushed to the side, barely touched on and virtually ignored. I think we have had enough of that feeling!

My partner and I fumbled along for several years. I read everything I could get my hands on and tried to create a relationship that wasn't full of chaos, resentment, and hurt. My partner, however, was not as enthusiastic as I was about learning how to fix 'our' ADHD issues, and I was struggling to find any sense of peace in my life.

Having done hours and hours of research discovering techniques, tips, taking classes, getting 3 types of coaching certifications, coaching clients and self improvement (still a work in progress) over the last 10 yrs I put this book together in the hopes of saving you some precious time and energy on how you can find some peace in your life.

So this book is for US, the **partners** of those with ADHD. This book is for the tired, burnt out, stressed out, pissed off, frustrated, resentful, hopeless and lost. In this book, I will aim to answer the questions; Can I find peace? Will it be lasting? And how in the Hell do I do this?

Greet the concepts with an open mind. Finding peace in any circumstance, and deciding to stay or leave from that place, is a beautiful thing. This book offers a new perspective on finding that peace within your relationship....YES, even if your partner never changes. Give it a try. After all, what you're doing right now isn't working, so why not DO IT DIFFERENTLY?

o ◉ CONNECT 4

Most of you are familiar with the game CONNECT 4.. In this game, each player chooses a color and then takes turns dropping colored tokens into a seven-column, six-row vertically suspended grid. The object of the game is to be the first to form a horizontal, vertical or diagonal line of four of one's own tokens. It is a 2 player game and the first player can ALWAYS win by playing the right moves.

Players in Connect 4 have perfect information; meaning there are no hidden elements in the game on either side. Much like Connect 4, this 'game' of partnership, each partner chooses how they are showing up (their token). You can always win by making the first move in your relationship. Learning how to show up with 'perfect information', not hiding anything, you can be your authentic self and allow your partner to do the same.

Every relationship is different, individual, and unique. Each partner brings with them a set of beliefs, attachment styles, and baggage from the past.

To define attachment styles or attachment bonds, they are the emotional connection(s) you formed as an infant with your primary caregiver and experiences in infancy and adulthood that contributed to these bonds.

There are 2 dominant styles, secure and insecure. Within the insecure attachment style, there are 3 subsets; Ambivalent or anxious, avoidant-dismissive and disorganized attachment.

Because attachment styles can have a tremendous effect on your current relationship, we will define each style briefly.

SECURE ATTACHMENT

When the primary caregiver conveyed safety and understanding to the infant, both physically and emotionally, the infant will have developed a secure attachment style.

As an adult that looks like a person who is self confident, trusting and hopeful. A person who can manage conflict, respond to intimacy, and deal with the ups and downs of romantic relationships.

Most of the population falls into the next category/categories because the perfect parent doesn't exist. So the chances that any of us have a 100% secure attachment style are pretty low.

INSECURE ATTACHMENT

When the primary caregiver was frightening or inconsistent, in emotional and/or physical response, one of the 3, or a combination of the 3 following insecure attachment styles, will be present.

1. Ambivalent or anxious attachment style individuals tend to be needy, often uncertain and lacking self esteem. Worried that others won't want to be with them, but craving emotional intimacy.

2. Avoidant-dismissive attachment style individuals are wary of intimacy and closeness and attempt to avoid emotional connection with others. They don't want to rely on others and do not want others to rely on them.

3. Disorganized/disoriented or fearful attachment styles stem from an intense fear,often because of childhood trauma, neglect or abuse. They feel they don't deserve love or closeness in relationships. Never learning how to self-soothe emotions, relationships and the world can feel unsafe and frightening.

Each of the styles contributes to the issues in relationships and to list all of those ways would take another book to cover it all. My advice here is, learn what your attachment style is, how it may be affecting your relationship, and learn how to transition to a more secure attachment style.

I'll leave you with some broad ideas as to how....

- Improve your nonverbal communication skills.
- Boost your emotional intelligence
- Develop relationships with people who are securely attached
- Resolve any childhood traumas

Our ADHD partners are just like us. Their attachment styles, which they bring to the table, resulted from their experiences with their parents and the environment.

And ADHD is rarely the only disorder present. Many times, there are comorbid disorders.

Some of the most prominent comorbidities; ODD (oppositional defiance disorder), OCD (obsessive-compulsive disorder), Depression, Anxiety, Learning disabilities, Language disabilities, motor skill difficulties, tic disorders and other psychological or neurological disorders. These contribute to your unique relationship.

So, while there are many similarities in relationships that are ADHD affected, they are also as diverse as each snowflake that falls from the sky. Take some time to reflect on your particular relationship by looking at your 'TOKENS' .

TOKEN 1-BELIEFS

What are some beliefs about relationships, about *your* relationship?

Do you believe that...
- Couples should never fight or that fighting is good so that you can get it all out? Or are you somewhere in between?
- Love (relationships) shouldn't be this hard?

- Your partner should be your best friend? With shared interests?
- Losing yourself in your partner is best?
- Your relationship is supposed to make you happy?
- If it's hard, it isn't right?
- Your partner should just know what you need?
- Or perhaps you believe it's ok to be brutally honest?
- You'll never get bored with your partner?
- Your partner (or you) should be without flaws?
- Everything should be 50/50?

These are just some examples of beliefs that you may have surrounding your relationship that may be making matters worse. False beliefs about relationships can lead to disappointment, toxicity, and unhealthy relationships with your partner and within yourself.

I brought a slew of false beliefs and distorted ideas of what a relationship SHOULD look like with me. On more than one occasion, I found myself feeling and saying, if this was meant to be, it wouldn't be this hard, at least not if it's the right relationship, and our relationship was anything but easy.

My beliefs came from too many fairytale movies and romantic 70's songs. I thought my partner would just know my every need, respond in what I deemed the correct way, and do things the way I would do them. It didn't cross my mind that we are each individual, with different upbringings, experiences, thoughts, desires, wants, and habits.

Beliefs are not always truths. We believe what we hear and the more we hear it (especially when it is our own voice) the more we believe. We use our personal experiences to validate our beliefs as well. Unfortunately, our perceptions are not as accurate as we think they are. Perception is not reality. Perception is simply the lens through which we filter reality.

Questioning beliefs helps to come to a more realistic view, and allows you to handle relationships with more mindfulness and care. That adds PEACE to the puzzle.

TOKEN 2-EDUCATION

Knowledge about ADHD. Educate yourself on the symptoms, how they present, and the comorbidities that can accompany ADHD.

Some say that knowledge is power…
KNOWLEDGE **ISN'T** POWER! Power is having, or capable of <u>exerting power</u>, potency, or influence. If you are looking for POWER in your relationship, you can stop reading right here. The knowledge needed is what you know or think you know about ADHD. Applied *knowledge that leads to understanding.*

Educating yourselves on ADHD, its symptoms, and how it shows up in your relationships will help you move from frustration, anger, and resentment into understanding, patience, love, and peace. Gaining knowledge isn't about helping your partner, it's to help yourself so that you can see through the shit, to calm down and focus on yourself for a change.

I had been studying everything I could find on ADHD, seeking to make sense of my life and relationship. And while there has been an increase in information on ADHD, it wasn't until listening to Dr Russell Barkley, in his lecture for parents of children with ADHD, The 30 Essential Ideas Every Parent Needs To Know, that it clicked with me as to what we were really dealing with. It was the start for me of being able to change my perspective on my partner and what effects ADHD truly had on my partner and our life.

If you haven't found Dr Russell Barkley, please look him up. With a multitude of credentials, he is an absolute authority on ADHD.

In one of his lectures, Dr Russell Barkley states that ADHD is a DISORDER of Executive Functioning. Most have seen this definition of ADHD but not considered what that really means, so let's break it down.

Disorder defined is an illness or condition that disrupts _normal_ physical or mental functions. ADHD is a mental disorder. It is a brain dysfunction.

A dysfunction is; an abnormality or impairment in the function of a specified bodily organ or system, or a deviation from the norms of social behavior in a way regarded as bad.

This may feel like doom and gloom to you, or be overwhelming, but it is not a death sentence, and you don't have to attach any feelings to this diagnosis. This is simply a definition of ADHD. These are just facts.

Gaining a realistic understanding of the true meaning of ADHD can help you to realize that this is a real impairment and not just a make-believe excuse for a person to have (what neurotypical people see as) wrong behaviors.

Realizing that my partner was born with a disability, much like if he was born without a leg or another physical attribute that we consider normal, I had better understanding and my empathy for him increased. Honestly, how could I be mad at him for having a disability and expect him to function like everyone else?

Would you expect a person born without legs to just get up and walk? NO, of course not. Could that person, with the help of technologies and outside help learn to use a wheelchair, or prosthesis or other means of moving around? ABSOLUTELY!

This realization that my partner was never going to outgrow or get rid of ADHD, and that this is a lifelong dysfunction that would require outside help (scaffolding), to hold his disability against him, holding him to expectation levels of what I considered 'normal' was, well, cruel and hurtful to not only him but to our relationship as well.

It can be a challenge, as with any mental disorder, to remember that there is one. Our partner looks normal, moves normally, and seems to function in the world, but there is a glitch in the matrix. When those glitches happen, it is easier to just react to them and want to change the person or circumstances than to help, reassure or be patient with them.

I got a firsthand education in this when I sustained a TBI or Traumatic Brain Injury in 2015. In my healing process, I looked fine, but my brain was on full melt down most days.

I struggled to focus and had incredible anxiety about going out into public. My short-term memory was strained and most of my recall of past events was gone. I was scared and exhausted most days but hid that shame or 'masked' because I thought others would see me as weird, weak and unintelligent. I felt misunderstood and alone.

It is an interesting fact; originally ADHD was categorized as a brain injury and from personal experience, a brain injury certainly has many of the same symptoms as ADHD.

If you look into types of ADHD, you will find that there are 3 basic types; hyperactive, inattentive, and combined. Some articles claim 4 types, some say 9…it can be overwhelming out in the 'web'. The most comprehensive list of types of ADHD that I have come across to date is Dr. Amen's 7 types of ADHD.

Dr. Amen has been studying ADHD for more than 20 yrs. We can find his research and results in his book, *Healing ADD: The Breakthrough Program That Allows You to See and Heal the 7 Types of ADD.*

I will list out the 7 types and encourage you to search out more information from Dr. Amen, where he lists out the causes of each type and the recommended treatment for each.

1. **Classic ADD**
Symptoms: Inattentive, distractible, hyperactive, disorganized, and impulsive. Normal brain activity at rest and decreased brain activity during concentrated tasks.

2. **Inattentive ADD**
Symptoms: Short attention span, distractible, disorganized, procrastinates, may daydream and be introverted; not hyperactive or impulsive; affects girls as much or more than boys.

3. Over-Focused ADD
Symptoms: Core symptoms of Classic ADD, plus trouble shifting attention. Going from thought-to-thought or task-to-task; getting stuck in negative thought patterns or behaviors.

4. Temporal Lobe ADD
Symptoms: Core symptoms of Classic ADD, as well as learning, memory, and behavioral problems, such as quick anger, aggression, and mild paranoia.

5. Limbic ADD
Symptoms: Core symptoms of Classic ADD, as well as chronic low-level sadness (not depression): moodiness, low energy, frequent feelings of helplessness or excessive guilt, and chronic low self-esteem.

6. Ring of Fire ADD ("ADD plus")
Symptoms: Sensitivity to noise, light, touch; periods of mean behavior; unpredictable behavior; speaking fast; anxiety and fearfulness.

7.Anxious ADD
Symptoms: Core symptoms of Classic ADD, as well as being anxious and tense. Having physical stress symptoms; headaches and stomachaches, predicting the worst, freezing in anxiety-provoking situations, especially if being judged.

The breakdown of the types of ADHD really helps to hone in on your particular situation and gives a better understanding of the particular issues your partner may be dealing with.

Another issue may be misinformation about ADHD. The internet is much like a public bathroom wall where anyone can write anything. There are many ideas, and myths about ADHD that have misled many and torn relationships apart.

Some *MYTH*understandings surrounding ADHD;

ADHD Myths...
- Isn't a real medical disorder.
- It is the result of bad parenting.
- Affects only boys.
- A person who has ADHD couldn't possibly sit and play games or, as an adult, sit through a visit.
- You will outgrow ADHD.
- People with ADHD are stupid or lazy or just need to try harder.
- Those who take medications for ADHD are more likely to abuse drugs.
- ADHD is a learning disability.
- ADHD means you get distracted by shiny objects (squirrels).

- Only kids can have ADHD, not adults.

These are just some myths. I'm sure we could all come up with more. The bottom line here is to gain accurate knowledge of what the disability is, how it shows up in their lives, and by association, yours as the non-ADHD person.

These Myth-understandings are a big reason our ADHDers grow up with so much shame and guilt, which can lead to a terrible self image. Those who were undiagnosed as a child or left untreated have suffered greatly because of these myths.

Imagine living your life without legs, people telling you to just try harder to walk, or assuming you could never be successful because of your condition. How about being denied help, whether it be medications or therapy to help you learn how to live in a world that isn't built for your disability?

Learning about ADHD is not about coming up with excuses for your partner's behaviors or to blame them for all your relational issues. Educating yourself on the symptoms of ADHD and how those symptoms may present themselves in your relationship will help you to create not only empathy, but an understanding that it's not personal, how to set healthy boundaries and add scaffolding to your lives, that can bring more harmony and peace. It is a process.

Take small bits of time in your day, look up an article on the internet, listen to podcasts about ADHD, join internet or in person support groups for ADHD partners. Watch quick videos and more. Keep updated on the latest finds and get a greater understanding of what you're dealing with.

TOKEN 3-SYMPTOMS

Let's go over some areas here in which ADHD symptoms can affect intimate relationships to help you get started on your journey of understanding.

So, WHERE DOES ADHD SHOW UP IN RELATIONSHIPS? AND HOW OFTEN?

EVERYWHERE!!! And ALL THE TIME!!!

That's right. For those that know, well, you know. ADHD symptoms do not discriminate. They show up in every area of a relationship and life and are present all the time. Name an area, name a time, it's there. Now there may be areas in which the symptoms are not interfering in a negative way, making them less noticeable or acceptable behaviors, but they are still there, nonetheless.

Knowing/learning what the symptoms are and how they may be showing up in your relationship is important because the better you get at recognizing them, the easier it becomes to handle the symptoms and your reactions to them. So while there is material out there to learn about the symptoms and how they may be affecting your relationship, we will still briefly cover them.

Hyper-focus, inattentiveness, distractibility, disorganization, forgetfulness, lack of social skills, lack of self awareness, impulsivity, time blindness, emotional dysregulation, chaotic lifestyle are some symptoms of ADHD.

ADHD is an executive function disorder. Executive function is the 'management system' of the brain. Imagine if you will, the brain as a business and the executive function as the managers of this business. The Managers have been hired to be responsible for 7 main areas of the business.

Those 7 main areas are;
- Self-awareness
- Inhibition and self-restraint
- Working memory
- Time management
- Self-control of emotions
- Self-motivation
- planning/problem solving

Managers are responsible for communicating with their team the proper way to carry out each of the responsibilities. As in most companies, there are skilled managers and crappy managers and everything in between. Some days, the managers may perform well, and sometimes they call in sick or just don't even show up for the day. How the manager decides to show up and serve their team each day has a great impact on the department and the company.

Using the example of a company, it is time for the quarterly review for managers. Here are some not so great things that may be on the review. *Disorganized, easily distracted, interrupts, forgets details, talks excessively, fails to follow instructions, loses things necessary for tasks, doesn't listen when spoken to directly, fails to give close attention to details, misses social cues, performs below one's abilities or intelligence level.

In their personal lives; erratic parenting styles, poor decision making, learned helplessness, low emotional intimacy, very low OR extremely high sex drive, impulsive spending, withdrawal, hypersensitivity to criticism, irritability, temper, lack of empathy, and poor self esteem may be displayed.

Another area, less talked about, is that those with ADHD are typically 35% more immature than others their age. As an example, handing a 16yr old person with ADHD the car keys is like handing an 11yr old the keys. Their maturity level does not reflect their physical age or abilities.

Those are just a few....overwhelming, I know. And with a performance like that in the workplace, most of those managers would get fired.

On the flip side, there are positive qualities that could be listed as well. Full of energy, handles emergencies well, thinks out of the box, is creative, works endlessly on a task that interests them, charming (makes the sale). And these may be enough to counteract the negatives and help the manager keep his position.

Now that you have a bit of an understanding on how the symptoms can show up, you can apply them into some areas of your personal life with your partner and begin to see where and how they may be manifesting. Here are some common issues for the partners in an ADHD relationship.

My partner….
- Fails to remember what I said
- Zones out during conversations
- Leaves a mess everywhere
- Leaves projects unfinished
- Talks without thinking
- Hurts my feelings
- Leaves all the finances up to me
- Spends money we don't have
- Forgets to pick up the kids or ignore them
- Leaves all the planning up on me
- Is irresponsible
- Gaslights me
- Is inconsistent
- Is controlling
- Has mood swings
- Is overly sensitive
- Is angry all the time
- Can't relax.

- Is avoidant

And the list goes on.

You can see how the symptoms are presenting and adding to the cycles in your relationships and you can choose new behaviors for yourself to break said cycles.

If you are anything like me, you are going to want to address it all and fix it asap. Patients, my lovely friends. You didn't get here overnight and you aren't going to fix it all overnight either. Choose one cycle to work on. Recognize them as they happen and begin to change your behaviors in the moment.

TOKEN 4-RESPONSIBILITY

There is a profound truth that you **need** to grasp and that is; in order to make a real, lasting difference in your life and your relationships, you must first take responsibility. Fully understanding and accepting (not approving or condoning or even loving) that you are in part responsible for the state of your relationship.

Logically, there are 2 halves of a relationship and you, my friend, are a half. You are responsible for your reactions, your emotions, your behavior, your beliefs and how you choose to show up in your relationship. Until you can accept responsibility (your response ability) you will remain stuck because you will never improve something that you don't feel responsible for.

But if I'm responsible, that means that it's my fault. That is just not true. If you get hit by a car, that is not your fault, but it is your responsibility to heal from any injuries. And in my personal experience with my sustained TBI (traumatic brain injury), it wasn't my fault that I was pushed off the bed, but it was my responsibility to heal and find ways to improve my brain and learn how to function in a new way.

It's not your fault you have a life filled with ADHD symptoms, but it is your responsibility to grow as a person and a partner, to learn how to improve YOUR quality of life and to find your own place of peace. It is your responsibility to improve your half of the relationship.

This isn't about changing or manipulating your partner. It's a journey within yourself. A journey to face **your** part in the negative cycles of your relationship and to find ways in which you can grow and find Joy in your relationship.

Although we are going to go through 'steps' in this book on finding peace, there is no defined starting or stopping point. Life is cyclical and in constant motion. Life is not linear, neither are the solutions to finding peace. Just start right where you are and grow with the information given as you go through the rise and fall, ups and downs and spinning circles of life.

♪ THE SONG THAT NEVER ENDS

This is the song that never ends.
It just goes on and on, my friend.
Some people started singing it, not knowing what it
was.
And, they'll continue singing it forever, just
because...

This is the song that never ends.
It just goes on and on, my friend.
Some people started singing it, not knowing what it
was.
And, they'll continue singing it forever, just
because...

This is the song that never ends...

(repeat forever)

Getting caught up in all the dysfunctional cycles in
your relationship can look and feel just like this
song. You started singing those dysfunctional songs
to one another, not knowing what it was, and if you
don't become aware of them, you'll sing them
forever, just because.

Awareness is the first step to all change!

At the very heart, or center of any change, there must be AWARENESS. I have seen many examples of 'wheels of change' and find they are lacking the center or the Hub. The Hub is the center that the rim attaches to and where the spokes meet. So before you get rolling down the street to peace town you must first begin by becoming aware of how you are showing up in the world, in your parenting, in your job, in your relationships.

I know, we've heard this before and like me you may have said, 'oh, I'm aware, aware that this relationship sucks.' 'I'm aware that my partner is an asshole.' 'I'm aware that I can't do this anymore.' 'I'm aware that she is too sensitive.' And many, many statements like that. Not exactly the awareness that we're talking about. The 'awareness' we are looking at here is the *quality* **or** *state of being* **aware**: knowledge and understanding that something is happening or exists.

There are 3 types of awareness:
1. Organizational awareness
2. Social awareness
3. Self awareness

1. Organizational awareness is important in a career, office politics and groups you belong to. Having awareness of the values and 'norms' that exist in those realms .

2. Social awareness is important in social situations; relationships you have with others. It's about understanding how you react in different social situations.

3. Self awareness is the ABILITY to know oneself. To have a DEEP understanding of what makes us *who* we are. The ability to see where we are, where we come from and where we are going as individuals.

Our focus is going to be on Self Awareness. Becoming self aware will help you in the social awareness and organizational awareness areas of life as well but the focus here is on Self.

So you might be saying, well shit, I thought I knew me! How could I not know me? I'm the only one who truly knows me. But when you look, REALLY look at yourself, is there an awareness of why you do the things you do? Why do you act the way you act? Where do your feelings flow from? What are your traumas and how do you relate to those? Where do your habits, quirks, and routines come from? What is your parenting style or why are you the spouse you are? Why do you eat what you eat? Why do you choose certain careers? And why did you choose the life partners that you did? Did you just get here on autopilot?

How do we get to this 'deep' understanding of what makes us who we are as individuals? First understand the 2 broad types of self awareness and then recognize and believe that you do have the ability to become self aware.

The 2 broad types of self awareness(S.A.) are *internal self-awareness* and *external self-awareness*.

Internal S.A.: How clearly we see our own values, goals, dreams, passions, reactions, thoughts, feelings, behaviors, strengths, weaknesses, and our impact on others.

External S.A.: How clearly we understand how other people view us in those same areas.

Do not assume that if you are aware in one area that you are also aware in the other areas.

To increase productive self awareness, ask WHAT not why. What questions help you to stay objective, future focused, and empower you to act on your newly found insights. For example, WHY does my partner not give me the attention I crave changes to WHAT do I need to do to have my need for attention met?

Get to know yourself. Look at your own attitudes, behaviors, expectations, hopes, dreams, concerns, behavior triggers, fears, etc. Doing some research, soul searching, and journaling will reveal things to you previously hidden (if you're open to it).

Facing your fears and delving into your own insecurities, distorted beliefs, and unhappiness provides the opportunity to be free from emotional dependence on another person. When you are emotionally dependent on your partner, you turn over your power and control to them. That can create a very scary and unsafe environment for you to be in.

Becoming aware, TRULY AWARE, of your thought life and taking responsibility for yourself, can move you from a place of fear to a place of peace.

When I started learning about ADHD, I became very excited about the information I was finding and was sharing with my partner all the things I was learning about how to help him with his ADHD. After all, I was excited to discover all the new and interesting things and how ADHD was affecting our relationship. It became the topic of conversation around our house. I would point out how he could be doing things differently or better. I was 'helping' him all the time, pointing out all the ways he could change the way he did things and his behavior. I really thought I was helping. My partner's perception was that I was being a control freak and forcing change on him that he didn't want nor ask for. This led us right into some unhealthy CYCLES AND PATTERNS.

BLAME. No I'm not, you are…

Depending on your particular set of circumstances, you may find yourself playing the blame game. In this cycle, partners blame each other for the issues in the relationship.

It isn't difficult to know if you are in the blame cycle. One or both partners are pointing a finger at the other, saying this is all your fault. Each person looks at the other as the bad guy/gal in hopes of a quick escape. Escape from guilt or responsibility or from feeling unworthy, unlovable or like a failure.

Blame is an easy way out, a way for you to continue your bad behavior. It's a denial of responsibility and keeps you from seeing ways in which you can alter your behavior to achieve a desired outcome. Blame leaves you powerless and keeps you from growing as individuals.

Blame is an unproductive cycle, where one partner blames and the other blames back and the wheel keeps turning. This cycle can often turn into name calling, hostility, resentments, backbiting, and other negative reactions. Both partners feel misunderstood and attacked. Blaming leads to resentment, anger and other negative emotions.

When issues arise, as they will, become aware of the words you are using. Things like, well, if you would have…. Or if you wouldn't have done that or said that… I did this because you did that. Or, that's just the way I am, or that's how I was raised. He made me feel…. Or she pressured me into it. Typically, these things will be negative in nature as there are few times when we blame others for our good feelings, thoughts, or behaviors. It can be a real eye opener when you notice the words coming out of your own mouth.

No one wants to see their own negative habits or behaviors, but it is imperative that you do.

Right now, just become an observer in your own life. Don't try changing anything yet...just become aware of your words and behaviors.

Ask yourself some questions. Am I feeling guilty? AM I feeling defensive? Do I have a need to be right? Am I afraid? If I am at fault, or wrong, what am I making that mean about me? What are the thoughts that you have, just before you speak or after the discussion or argument?

Answering these questions in a journal may be helpful. Writing it down will help to bring about some awareness and take your thoughts and actions out of the subconscious mind and bring it into the conscious mind.

Once you become aware, face the 'ugly' within yourself. That's where you begin to break the cycles. That is where your power lies.

This might be causing some push back from you, I get it. I used to feel like if my partner would just change, work on himself, stop blaming me and putting me on the defensive, then I could relax and stop blaming him.

I used to think it was ALL on my partner. After all, I wasn't like this before we got together. Even while reading ADHD centered marriage/relationship books, I felt justified in blaming him for all our issues. I mean, he's the one with ADHD, not me, right? I failed to realize that because I lacked a true understanding of ADHD, and my particular partner, that I had fallen into just reacting to the symptoms of ADHD instead of understanding them and learning how to navigate through them.

Once you have become aware you are participating in the blame cycle and understand the emotions behind it you can be on the lookout for your patterns and begin to change them.

Learning how to communicate your truth is crucial in this process. You don't have to lash out, yell back, be defensive or hurtful to be heard. Yes, this is going to take time, self discipline and practice. Be loving, kind, and forgiving of yourself as you go through the process.

A simple practice in all areas of communication is to 'practice the pause'. Pause before talking. JUST BREATHE! You have the ability to choose what you say, how you react, and how you feel. And again, no, this isn't easy and can require continuous effort through the years.

Breathe, check in with yourself. What are you feeling? What are your thoughts? What words do you want to speak? Are those things serving you? Meaning, what is your desired outcome and are these things going to bring you closer or farther away from that outcome?

Helpful hints;
Saying things (in a calm tone) such as;
I feel statements…
I feel defensive. I feel anxious. I feel misunderstood. I feel triggered. I feel scared. Can help both you and your partner to understand what is happening in this cycle and to calm down a bit. By recognizing and stating what feelings you are experiencing, you will then be able to show up in a healthier way.

Keep in mind that when you blame another you are giving up your responsibility, **response ability** (our ability to respond as we would choose).

One statement that helped me to remember that we were in this together was 'Same team'. This

41

statement was my partner's idea to say to one another when we would get riled up or in a heated discussion and blame started to creep in.

But what if my partner isn't willing to change or participate in this? Then tell yourself! Remind yourself, 'we're on the same team'. It can diffuse the anger and defensiveness you may be feeling just to say that in your own head, helping you to become solution focused, which is another helpful tip, stay SOLUTION FOCUSED.

Shifting the focus onto what the desired outcome you want will help stop the blame game. Become curious. Curious about your partner, about why they are blaming, about what is underneath their words. This can help you to understand them more fully. Ask questions, in a curious, not accusing way to gain more understanding about your partner, their words and actions.

Owning your part in the problem straight away, admitting what is your fault, is a great way to diffuse an argument and stop the blaming. Be careful to not take blame for what is not yours, a martyr is not the goal and serves no one and blaming doesn't either. Own your part, ask for forgiveness or make the apology and offer future change on your behalf.

Also, keep in mind that in order to stop the cycle, you may need to step away from the conversation. Do not just storm off. Make a statement about your need to step away from the conversation and that you can address it when you are in a better frame of mind. We will cover more on this in the setting healthy boundaries section.

Blaming can piggyback off of or look like another cycle that Mellissa Orlov calls the …

SYMPTOM -RESPONSE-RESPONSE CYCLE

In this cycle, an ADHD Symptom may create a misunderstanding or misinterpretation. A corresponding response to that symptom from the non-ADHD partner follows, which then creates a misunderstanding or misinterpretation and a corresponding response to that response by the ADHD partner.

Yes, I see the cycle starts with the symptom. The only one that can address the actual symptom is the partner with ADHD. However, this book is about when your partner is not addressing their symptoms and what you can do from your side of the table. It is your 'interpretation' of said symptom and your response to it, where you have control and can stop this cycle. Becoming more aware of the symptoms of ADHD and recognizing them when and where they show up in your relationship will give you the foundations you need. Once you notice the symptoms (yes, at first this takes effort, but after some time practicing this, it will become easier to identify the symptoms that are specific to your person and relationship) you get to choose how you respond to them. Let's go through an example of this.

Example 1:
An ADHD partner picks up their phone in the middle of a conversation and starts checking messages or social media. The non-ADHD partner gets angry at the rude behavior and feels as if their partner doesn't care about them. The non-ADHD partner responds by leaving the area, making nasty comments, yelling, crying…., the ADHD partner is shocked back into the moment and doesn't understand what is happening and gets defensive and chooses their response to the situation, typically in a negative way.

Example 2:
An ADHD partner picks up their phone in the middle of a conversation and starts checking messages or social media. The non-ADHD partner

realizes their partner heard a notification from their phone and is now distracted. Instead of responding from a place of hurt and anger, the non-ADHD partner understands this isn't personal and uses their partner's name or a gentle touch to 'snap' them back into the present moment. Asking nicely if they need a minute to answer or check the notification or if it can wait until after they are done with the current conversation. The ADHD partner can now respond to the question however they choose (hopefully nicely).

In example 2 the non-ADHD partner has changed the symptom-response-response cycle from a negative one into a more positive interaction.

Plug this action into your situations and see how changing your response can change the negative patterns in your relationship.

PARENT/CHILD

Ooh...this one right here hits home big time! Being a mother of 3 boys and homeschooling them prior to meeting my partner made it easy for me to fall into the role of parenting him. Not to mention, he enjoyed being taken care of and well mothered (to an extent). So this interaction became a norm in our home for years. Not that it went over well, more like we both just became apathetic to the pattern and felt that it would never change.

I thought my partner was incompetent, immature and would never grow up to be an 'adult' in life. This was based on my own misinterpretations of ADHD symptoms. His inability to organize and prioritize, to complete boring tasks, his immaturity, zoning out, and impulsive behaviors, led to these thoughts.

He decided it's easier to let me do things for him and not argue or cause issues about it all. This led us both into incredible resentment towards one another. Seething in anger, both of us shut down or lashed out, depending on the day.

It is an easy dynamic to fall into, especially in an ADHD affected relationship. Compensating for what you see as weaknesses in your ADHD partner is usually where this starts. You see a symptom that looks like immaturity and irresponsibility, so you take on said responsibility. This process repeats and repeats until you find yourself taking on most of the responsibilities and your ADHD partner is seemingly just having fun and not caring. Cue the nagging and reminders to do their chores, pay the bills, pick up after themselves, put gas in the car, mow the lawn and all the other 'duties' you deem necessary. And just like a rebellious teenager, they fuss, fight, shut down, or are downright disrespectful.

Notice your thoughts. The misinterpretations of ADHD symptoms, thoughts you have about them, create your feelings and actions towards your partner.. Are you misinterpreting symptoms as character traits and parenting them?

Some signs that you have taken on the parenting role in your relationship can look like:
- demeaning interactions
- disrespect for your partner
- inflexibility
- financial control
- unrealistic expectations.

There are situations in which you take on the parenting role because it offers you some sense of meaning. As an example, after raising my own children, I found myself a bit lost. Once I realized they no longer needed me, it was easy to turn that mothering attention onto my partner. It fulfilled a need in me to be a caretaker and oddly enough, I then blamed and resented my partner for the role that I took on.

If you continue to do things for your partner, things they can do for themselves, you are only hurting them. You are sending the message that you believe they cannot function without you, that they are incompetent.

Self- growth is a way to reveal to us our reason(s) why we act the way we do and gives great insight into our choices and how to break our cycles and make healthier choices and live more authentically. That journey is a much needed journey and can only improve your life and your relationships. It is a journey that would require an entire book to delve into. Perhaps that will be a future one that I will write, but for now, back to the task at hand.

My goal as a parent was to raise a contributing member of society and my mantra was 'momma ain't always going to be there'. My children needed to learn basic life skills and learn how to function in the world in which they live. So too, do our partners. Just like a supportive parent, you can be a supportive partner without being the helicopter parent…I mean, partner. While you may typically enjoy caring for others, your actions may be seen as controlling, disguised as 'helping'.

Being supportive allows you to let go of the responsibility for another person's choices, thoughts, and behavior. READ THAT STATEMENT AGAIN.

Switching from a mindset of parenting your partner to supporting your partner, you can relax into the relationship, instead of feeling like the relationship is a burden.

Being supportive looks like asking your partner what they need help with and, more importantly, asking HOW you can help. It looks like letting them fail and not fixing it for them. It looks like stepping out of the tornado of chaos and being calm in the storm.

While parenting your partner is not the intent, it helps to remember that there is that tender child in all of us. We typically wouldn't yell at our kid for not knowing how to do something or for doing it differently than we would. We wouldn't take things over because we didn't like how they did it or that it wasn't done in our time frame. You wouldn't withhold love, affection, attention or be unkind. You wouldn't nag them or lash out with verbal abuse. You wouldn't embarrass or belittle them in front of friends or family. You most definitely wouldn't interpret your child's actions to mean anything about us. You wouldn't take it personally. And yet this is exactly what happens in our romantic relationships.

You can learn to come alongside them, ask if they need help or clarification. You can approach the situation with a curious mind instead of a demanding and controlling mindset. You can encourage when they have small accomplishments and console or hold space for them in their failures. You can be more patient and understanding with them. Instead of blaming and shaming. You can acknowledge your part in this dynamic and take responsibility for your behavior. You can be more direct and polite in your requests for help. And you can learn to communicate more clearly about your needs.

Just because you see an adult in front of you, who appears to be 'normal', what you are not seeing is the brain function that is impaired. And hell yes, that shit is hard to remember. But training your mind to remember that there IS a dysfunction can help you calm your reactions and better handle the ADHD ups and downs.

Conversely, while not typical in ADHD relationships, occasionally the non-ADHD partner will fall into the 'child' side of the cycle.

You may be a person who really enjoys being taken care of, or perhaps you have a more avoidant attachment style where you withdraw from conflict. Another reason that you may have fallen into the child role is a passive aggressive pattern in order to attempt to control the chaos. It may also be due to not having healthy boundaries. You may have been raised with parents that took care of everything for you and created that expectation. Whatever the case, if you find yourself in this role, do not be surprised to notice your ADHD partner is frazzled and exhausted as the parent role they find themselves in is completely draining their executive functioning.

Finding your reasons for your part as the child in this cycle will lead you to the fix. Set firm boundaries. Find ways in which you can fill your own needs and be less reliant on your partner. Take on tasks that you can complete and follow through on them. Be more direct instead of passive-aggressive with your partner. A good guide to remember, if I can do this myself, do it. If I truly need help, ask for it.

When you find yourself in the parent/child dynamic and at some point you will, it is necessary to recognize the pattern and stop your part in the dynamic. Before you offer advice, take over a project or task, ask yourself, am I parenting my partner or leaving it all up to my partner? Is this serving our relationship? Is this going to increase or decrease our ability to function as partners? Allow your partner to contribute in their own way. Learn how to soothe your own anxiety and establish healthy boundaries. (we will cover these processes later in this book).

Another helpful tip I personally used is to ask myself, 'would I want my partner... talking to me that way, treating me like that, talking about me like that to our peers, putting all those restrictions and responsibilities on me, or handing me a chore list?' At a basic level, it's the old 'treat others the way you want to be treated.'

CHORE WARS

Now here is an area where the parent/child dynamic can really flare up. As a non-ADHD partner, you may find you're frustrated knowing that you really don't want to come off as nagging or being bossy all the time. Or you may feel let down, unable to trust your partner with requests because you never know if they are going to get completed or not. You may work from home full time and can therefore be responsible for more of the household tasks. Perhaps it's a matter of traditional role expectations as to why the tasks are split the way they are. And in most relationships, the higher percentage of household chores goes to the feminine half even if they work outside of the home. Whatever your situation, look into where your beliefs and perceptions on household responsibilities came from, find out what you really value in this area. And as we let go of our expectations on chores/tasks, new solutions appear.

Much of the traditional expectations come from our upbringing and society as a whole, and it is absolutely ok to choose to do most of the housework, or to be the primary one who does a certain task. Perhaps you like things done a certain way and anything outside of that makes you cranky or irritable. There is no right or wrong way to divide up chores, but trying to bend someone to live by another's standards is unfair at best.

If you find yourself resentful because you quietly have taken on most of the chores, then it's time to reevaluate your role. Acknowledge you may have done this to yourself through criticizing your partner's way of doing something or by assuming that they wouldn't or couldn't do it themselves. Addressing these issues first with yourself and then, with a clear mind about how you even got to this point, address the issues with your partner.

Having an honest discussion about what will work for you both and in your household is the best way to navigate through the chore wars. Be SOLUTION focused in the conversation. Decide what tasks need doing, what tasks each person's strengths are better suited for and when each person prefers to work on them. Don't forget if there are children in the home they too can pitch in and help. Delegating tasks to each child at their maturity and skill level not only takes some of the burden off but it also teaches kids important life skills and that a family is a team and each team member contributes to the success of the home.

Coming up with alternative solutions, such as hiring out things that neither person wants to do, and you can afford, can lighten the load for both of you. Figure out what each person's strengths and weaknesses are and come up with solutions that will work for both of you. Try to not be rigid in your ways, allowing for different solutions to be ok too. Give time for new habits to form and learn to let others help and make mistakes.

An idea to consider is that each person is 100% responsible for specific tasks. It is hard to delegate ½ of a task. It's either your task or my task. When you do 100% of a task, chore or job and it doesn't get done, then we know who hasn't done it; there's no debate. My partner doesn't tell me how to do my tasks, nor does he tell me when to do them. It is my choice. It is something I control. And likewise, I no longer need to tell him to do his tasks or how to do them. It is his responsibility. Once you have chosen a task and take full responsibility for that task, it brings freedom from blame, shame, and parenting.

As partners, when one person, because of a medical reason or travel or other factors, cannot complete their tasks, 'picking up the slack' for one another, in a loving way, benefits the entire household and relationship.

PURSUER/DISTANCER CYCLE

The closer I get, the farther away you are. Sound familiar? This is a normal way to navigate in a relationship under stress, however, this becomes a problem when it is entrenched in your everyday interactions.

Both individuals can take turns in these roles at different times in the relationship. Pursuers want intimacy and are often unaware of their need for autonomy. A Distancer wants autonomy and they are often unaware of their need for intimacy. Whichever role you find yourself in, developing a bit of the opposite quality will bring balance; balance between togetherness and separateness.

The pursuer in a relationship usually sees themselves as the more committed, self aware, emotionally developed, partner. Pursuers are usually seen by others as the righteous martyrs. Who are only looking for more intimacy in a relationship and not getting the appreciation they so deserve (in their mind), for their heartfelt efforts. The distancing partner may see them as desperate and clingy. For the pursuer there are what may seem like rewards for being the pursuer. They may discover that they have control over the level of intimacy and vulnerability in the relationship. When they want some attention they pursue; when they want space, they don't initiate. Winning the appreciation or pity of their friends and family, or getting a reputation for being a hard-working partner who sacrifices everything, can give them a sense of self-importance.

The reality is, the pursuer is left feeling unappreciated and taken for granted. They experience a deep sense of rejection. Often left with a feeling of a lack of love, intimacy, and eroticism. Low self esteem ensues.

Pursuing is typically seeking external soothing from others. Learn to self-soothe and meet your own emotional needs. Yep, the answer is, stop pursuing. I know it's scary as hell. Been there! We're afraid if we stop pursuing them, they will leave us. And…they might. That is a chance that you must be willing to take. And if you really think about it, do you want someone to stay with you because they feel trapped? Or do you want someone to stay because they choose to stay? You will most likely find that once you stop pursuing and the pressure is taken off your partner that they can stop running away.

Learning to self soothe will go a long way in helping you to break this cycle. Using self-talk to work through uncomfortable or scary feelings is incredibly useful. Reassuring yourself that is only a feeling and feelings are not going to kill you. Self-talk such as 'I am safe, I'm ok' when you feel those feelings that make you want to pursue.

Become aware of how it feels in your body. For example, when I feel insecure, my shoulders droop, my body feels heavy, there is a sick feeling in my stomach and I just want to hide. Just sit with those sensations. They are simply vibrations in the body.

Now ask yourself what are your thoughts surrounding these emotions. Check those thoughts with a question...**Is it true?** True as in, can that thought be proven in a court of law? If it is true...SO WHAT? So what, not as in, so what no one cares but more in a way of so what happens if that is true? Worst case scenario. Then process that and ask yourself if that happened, will I be ok? Most of the time, you will find that you are safe, it'll be ok, and you will survive. There is no emotion that can kill you.

Another way to self soothe is by giving yourself what you are hoping to get from your partner. If it's love you need, love yourself by doing something that makes you feel loved. Need attention? Give yourself attention. Go get your nails done, do something in the line of self care. Listen to your favorite music, dance, go for a bike ride or walk. It's not about buffering by avoiding these feelings, but instead acknowledging your needs and giving them to yourself. When you get in tune with your needs and stop depending on others to see them and fulfill them, you can operate from a place of wholeness and stop the pursuing cycle.

The distancer usually sees themselves as superior to the pursuer who is constantly begging for intimacy and attention. Others view the distancer as independent, bold, and strong. The pursuer may see them as cold, uncaring, and mean.

The rewards for the distancer are the feelings that being constantly pursued gives them. It makes the distancer feel desirable, gives them a sense of security that they won't be abandoned and ultimately gives them a sense of control in a relationship. The reality is the distancer feels like they can't show any need for intimacy or affection, which leads to an incredible sense of loneliness.

The distancer struggles with being able to voice their needs. They become quiet in the relationship and avoidant. Which leads to criticism from their partner and they withdraw even more.

If you are the distancer, stop distancing! You do this by connecting to your loneliness and understanding what it means to you to be vulnerable.

It can be scary to confront your vulnerability and see that you actually desire a closeness with your partner. You may feel weak or even silly about this need, but at its basic level, it is a human need.

Check your thoughts on being vulnerable. Do you think it makes you weak? Are you afraid that your partner may use your vulnerability against you? Where do these thoughts come from? And as in the example above, put them to the 'is it true' test and 'so what' analogy.

Practice feeling your feelings. Take time to put aside the buffers and avoidance tools and learn to first be vulnerable with yourself. Start with just a few moments each day and work your way up to longer periods of time where you can 'be still, and know'. Know yourself, know your energy, know that you are safe. Accept that your feelings are just that, feelings. Emotions are not to be feared, they are simply ENERGY IN MOTION, processing through your body.

When you can sit with your emotions and not judge them, it is easier to let others see those emotions as well. Learn to speak up and state your needs in a loving way. Draw closer to your partner by scheduling time to connect or be intimate, such as date night, Sunday breakfast, mid week lunch or an evening walk. Finding ways to connect without feeling cornered by doing an activity together is often helpful. Set healthy boundaries surrounding your desired alone time and give yourself the space you need to recharge.

Both the pursuer and distancer will benefit by taking care of their own needs and by becoming curious, instead of judgemental, about their partner's needs.

WALKING ON EGGSHELLS

Both partners can feel like they are walking on eggshells around the other. Each person anticipating the other's reactions and emotions. The non-ADHDer is on edge, never knowing what they can expect from their ADHD partner. It may be kindness, it may be rudeness, maybe they forget to do that thing they promised or maybe it gets done halfway. Perhaps they are kind, loving, and sweet, only to explode unexpectedly over some small frustration. It is unnerving, to say the least, when you're guessing what behavior you may experience in their presence. And similarly, the ADHD partner may be walking on eggshells trying to please their partner and never feeling like what they do is right because they are constantly criticized and worried about making their partner angry, anticipating the non-ADHDers response to everything.

There are other factors that can play into this as well. If there is an addiction, personality disorder, anxiety or depression, these issues need to be addressed in order to rebuild trust and safety in the relationship.

Emotional dysregulation in those with ADHD is very real and affects not only this cycle, but all areas of life for them. Emotional dysregulation is an impaired ability to control emotional response. 2 main causes for this in the ADHD brain: an overactive amygdala and underactive frontal cortex.

The amygdala is the part of the brain that triggers emotional response. So you can see if you have an overactive amygdala that emotions will tend to be stronger than they would be to a neurotypical person.

The frontal cortex is responsible for filtering and inhibiting emotions so that you can react to triggers in a more 'socially acceptable' manner. If the frontal cortex is underactive it is not inhibiting emotional reactions.

Some of the signs to of Emotional dysregulation include:

- Reactions that seem out of sync with their cause
- Difficulty calming down
- Low tolerance for frustration
- Prone to sudden outbursts
- Feeling completely overwhelmed
- Difficulty in refocusing attention away from an emotion

With emotional dysregulation, walking on eggshells around your partner feels safer than the alternative.

Sometimes, your **unhealthy attachment** to one another is the culprit. Many of you fall into the, when our relationship is good, it's really good, but when it's bad, it's really bad. You hold on during the really bad times in hopes of feeling the good ones again. This, oh, this was us!

You may stay in the eggshell cycle because of **guilt**, thinking it must be me.thinking, 'I'm doing something wrong'. It may be low self esteem too. Or perhaps you are caught up in people pleasing mode. Find your root cause(s), process them. Be honest with yourself and accept (not approve of) your issues and work to deal with them so you can come from a place of maturity and strength.

Start clearing the eggshells by first stopping your efforts to make the other person feel a certain way. No matter what your actions are, you are only responsible for your actions. You cannot make them think or respond in a certain way. It is their choice and responsibility. Unless you are an all powerful wizard, their mood is their problem. And that goes both ways. Your mood is your problem.

Live from your authenticity. Get centered and go with your gut. Stop second guessing your actions. If you are constantly living in a state of unrest, your partner senses this and it only makes them feel like something is off as well and there you go, walking on eggshells again. Healthy boundaries, setting them and respecting others', will play a large part in stopping this cycle as well.

ANGER AND RESENTMENT

This cycle is more like a cyclone than just a cycle and there are layers upon layers to go through here.

Let's start with anger. Anger comes in many forms and for many reasons. In order to not spend most of our time delving into all the areas, reasons, and solutions for anger, let's stick as closely as we can to how it relates in our ADHD affected relationships. Keep in mind, we are addressing our ½ of the cycle here, and that is all we can control.

Anger is just the tip of the iceberg. We know that an iceberg is a large floating mass of ice and it is understood that what is seen above the waters line is only a small portion of the actual ice mass, that underneath the water is a much larger mass of ice that remains hidden. So too is anger. Anger is an emotion, a secondary emotion, meaning there are primary emotions that are found underneath, just like the iceberg.

Some of the primary emotions that lie underneath the tip of the anger iceberg are sadness, disappointment, stress, hurt, insecurity, overwhelm, tired, anxious, hungry, lonely, threatened, pain, contempt, guilt, embarrassment, scared, helplessness, jealousy, and shame. I'm certain you can come up with some others when you start to discover what lies underneath your iceberg.

Where the anger started for each of us is different. Maybe, shortly after the hyperfocus of the beginning of your relationship wore off, you found yourself dazed and confused?. Losing that wonderful feeling, without seeing any cause for that to happen, can leave you feeling angry. Perhaps what you saw as immaturity, irresponsibility, or avoidant behavior led to your anger. Or was it the weight of the world on your shoulders of handling all the responsibilities that brought you to anger? Sometimes you get angry that you're seemingly angry all the time. You get angry at yourself too, for all sorts of reasons. Perhaps, like me, it's all the above and more.

Anger, in and of itself, is not a 'bad' emotion. As a matter of fact, there is not any emotion that is either bad or good. Remember, emotions are energy in motion, vibrations in the body. Energy can have a high or low vibration in the body and can result in different results within you. Without getting all foo-foo and mystical here, anger is neither good nor bad, it just is.

Anger is a protector of raw emotions. I love that description. When you see anger as a protector, it changes your perspective on it. Another way anger can be seen as a protector is to imagine a large adult. An adult who is strong and fearless, the warrior, and behind this 'warrior', is a large gathering of children of all ages and sizes. The children are terrified and look to the warrior to protect them from having to step out and confront their fears.

Anger can show you areas within yourself that you need to work on. Anger can be a signal that your environment is wrong for you. Anger can show you that boundaries of yours are getting crossed or that you are crossing other's boundaries. Step out from behind the warrior and be seen.

What is underneath your tip of the iceberg? Who is that you are hiding behind the warrior? Take time to think about it, write it down, yell it into a pillow...whatever it takes to purge that vibration of anger, processing it and releasing it to see what lies beneath the waters for you. Put on that scuba gear.

Let's look at some situations where anger may pop up in our relationships.

I get angry or I feel angry;
Literally all the time and about everything may be your response. But, let's dive in.

I feel angry;
- When my partner doesn't help with chores.
- When my partner does finally help with chores but does it wrong.
- When my partner says one thing and does another.
- When I'm left with all the planning and responsibilities.

- When my partner forgets… important dates, to pick up items from the store, to do the one little thing I asked for,to pay the bills, or pick up the children and on and on.
- When my partner talks down to me or is mean to me.
- When my partner tunes out and just plays video games or hides in their phone.
- When my partner is the life of the party but a party pooper at home.
- When my partner has 10k+ projects going on and nothing is complete.

I get angry at myself;
- For settling in this relationship.
- For being blindsided and feeling duped.
- For accepting poor treatment from my partner.

And the list goes on.

Write your 'I feel angry when' list down. It will help you process the anger and lead you to a place where you can then discover what is really under the water for you.

When anger pops up, be aware. Feel it in your body. Describe it to yourself. Notice how and where it is vibrating in your body. Sit with it for a time. Your timing will be different from others', so be patient with yourself. I have found the more I do this, the quicker the process becomes.

In a heated moment of conversation with your partner, it may be a good time to request a time out with a confirmation that you can continue the chat at a later time. It is always helpful to set up that time right then.

Once you can be alone for a few moments, ask yourself some questions about your anger. Become curious as to what the protector is trying to tell you. Is it the child of helplessness, overwhelm, or hurt? Is it those other kids, embarrassment or scared? Maybe it's sadness, hopelessness or disappointment? Once you can find the children hiding or that 'primary emotion', you can then process it through your body in the same way you learned to process anger; feel it in your body, describe it to yourself, and sit with it for a time.

Writing your thoughts down here is helpful, even if all it looks like is the word fuck written all over the page. Trust me, it's therapeutic.

Now that you have a clear, or at least a less muddled, idea of what is hiding behind the anger, you will be able to have a conversation with your partner that is less heated on the subject. And sometimes you realize that you are no longer feeling the things that led to the anger and the issues just resolve themselves. Be honest about that with your partner too.

Letting those emotions come out from behind the warrior and seeing them for who and what they are gives you the opportunity to give to yourself. Perhaps there is a boundary that needs shearing up. You may need to speak your truth more. Are there areas where you are expecting your partner to just read your mind or fulfill something within you that you could be fulfilling for yourself? Are you worried about what others may think or say? And one of my favorites...are you trying to control everything? That was the source of most of my anger and frustration.

Become mindful of the emotions under the water and begin to ask yourself what you need in this situation to feel calm again. Anger only begets anger. Getting in tune with what your true emotion is will give you the insight and help you plan a better resolution for the issue.

SEXUAL ISSUES
Oh yeah, baby!

The dreaded subject. One in which most books on ADHD do NOT dare cover. Kudos to Ari Tuckman for tackling this topic in his book ADHD After Dark.

There are two reported sexual symptoms of ADHD; HYPER-sexuality and HYPO-sexuality. Hyper means the ADHDer may have a higher than the average bear, sex drive, while Hypo means interest in sex can be like watching grass grow.

While these, at their most intense, are serious psychiatric disorders that require a specialist, we are going with the notion that your partner is not to that point in either direction. If you suspect that they may have a serious psychiatric disorder, guide them to a therapist that can help them.

It's common to have unmatched sex drives, with one partner wanting more sex and the other wanting less, now entering stage left...ADHD. Remember, we talked about where ADHD symptoms can show up and the answer was everywhere and all the time? Yeah, well, your sex life is no exception to this. And yeah…that can suck donkey balls!

Sex drive is the biological need. It encompasses both anatomical and neuroendocrine-physiological responses to sexual thoughts or stimuli. While sexual desire is the wish to engage in sexual activity. There are so many contributing factors to both hyper and hypo-sexuality that we cannot possibly address them all here.

Some contributing factors for both sides of the sexual issues from the AHDH standpoint can be;
Medications (or the lack thereof)
Impulsivity
Distraction
Boredom
Lack of communication
Pornography
Brain fatigue
Time management
Let's not forget all the cycles of the ADHD relationship that result in hurt feelings, anger, resentment, and controlling behaviors.
There is a correlation between sexual frequency, sexual satisfaction, and overall relationship satisfaction.

While we can focus on desire and frequency, preferences, pornography uses, open relationships and monogamy, drive is going to be our focus here. There are books, articles, videos, and so much more on both sides of this that connect the dots where you can find more answers on sexual issues, physical reasons for them, techniques and even on the ADHD and sexual issues front. Just know that ADHD symptoms are definitely at play here.

From a medical standpoint, the list can go on and on. Not every situation falls into these categories. There are many facets to sexual relationships and we cannot possibly discuss all the options, opinions, and issues surrounding this. Both hyper and hypo have attachment styles, along with childhood trauma, religious backgrounds, and many other factors that contribute to each condition. Looking into those areas may require some research on your part out there on the internet.

If you find that this is an area of great struggle for you and your partner, please seek out a professional therapist who specializes in sexual issues and....I repeat AND also understands ADHD. Ruling out any medical or physical contributors is always helpful. So assuming there are no medical or other physical contributors here, let's move on.

In looking at the definitions of desire versus drive, I believe the desire is there for both Hyper and Hypo; it's the drive that differs. Both 'wish' to have sex, but the drive varies. Drive comes from self motivation coupled with ambition. You can see it right there, how ADHD may affect this area. Self motivation is an executive function and those with ADHD have a deficit in executive functioning. On one side, the lack of being able to control that motivation (impulsivity) and on the other struggling to get motivated (task paralysis).

Biologically, sex hormones are associated with neurotransmitters that regulate libido or sex drive. Those neurotransmitters rely upon estrogen, testosterone, progesterone, oxytocin, serotonin, norepinephrine, acetylcholine, and dopamine. Dopamine is lacking in those with ADHD....hello?! Someone with hyper sex drive may be chasing that dopamine while someone with hypo sex drive may be severely lacking it and feel unmotivated.

If you find yourself in a HYPER-sexual relationship, you can sometimes feel overwhelmed by the demands on you and your body. And yes, you can feel this way no matter if you are the feminine or masculine half. I have seen many men who cannot 'keep up' with their partner's sex drive and feel completely exhausted and embarrassed at this discovery. It isn't always the masculine that has a higher drive,so let's drop that stereotype right now.

Hyper-sexuality means you or your partner have an unusually high sex drive. This is different from a desire for sex. Some ppl with ADHD are hypersexual, leading to increased sexual behaviors that are high risk, not appropriate(as deemed by society), or problematic. Sometimes they are labeled as sex addicts. Why might we find this issue with ADHD partners? Their need for stimulation, newness, escapism, anxiety relief, impulsivity, and distractibility all plays a part. The hyper-sexual brains get a kick from the endorphins that mobilize the neurotransmitters in the brain and it can actually help the ADHD brain to feel a sense of calmness and reduce restlessness. It's a bit like taking medication for ADHD when you look at it through this lens.

Making a change with a partner who is more on the HYPER-sexual spectrum is going to take you setting some healthy boundaries with your partner.

Personal autonomy is a thing. Personal autonomy defined is engaging in behavior by choice. It is a person's prerogative to determine when, with whom and under what circumstances they engage in sexual activity; to only engage in sexual activity to which they consent. This is not a word to be thrown around as a reason to never have sex with your partner again. It is a starting point of you realizing that your body is your own and you have dominion over that body.

Having a discussion with your partner about your boundaries (that we will learn how to set), finding balance between each of your needs and having a willingness to experiment, or be a bit more adventurous is a wonderful place to start.

If you find yourself in a HYPO-sexual relationship, you can sometimes feel lonely, depressed, and unloved. Hypo-sexuality means you or your partner have an unusually low sex drive. Sometimes this happens even if you desire sex, there just isn't the drive to actually go through with it. Some people with ADHD are HYPO-sexual because of their medicine, intimacy issues, sheer exhaustion, lack of concentration or interest, and sometimes because of over sensitivity issues to smells, touch, lighting and sounds. Distractibility also can play a factor and be misinterpreted by their partners as disinterest.

Making a change with a partner who is more on the HYPO-sexual spectrum is also going to take setting some healthy boundaries with your partner. Expressing your need to your partner and finding out what may be hindering their drive and finding ways to balance both will be a great starting point for you. Creating an atmosphere that is safe, fun and offers reward (other than orgasm) can increase motivation.

I believe that both issues are 1 side of the same coin. That coin being connection and intimacy. Both sides have a desire for connection and intimacy AND a fear of connection and intimacy.

Let's take Hyper-sex. Hyper has a need for connection with his partner, but has a fear of forming close relationships with others. Insecurity in self lies under that hyper exterior. Sex itself becomes a way to escape the negative feelings and low self esteem. It also gives them, if only temporarily, the much desired connection. Sex is a way for Hyper to 'feel' as if there is a sense of intimacy without actually becoming intimate on an emotional level. Hypo tends to be the more avoidant type. The fear of intimacy is there, but the thought is that if they don't connect sexually, then they can reduce the risk of intimacy happening. The need for connection is still there and they may find other ways to 'feel' connected or give the illusion of connection through shared activities or other avenues outside of sex. Hypo too has a low self esteem and avoiding sex is their escape.

Begin with this understanding of where your partner may be at, take ADHD into consideration and start to improve your sex life. I am in no way saying that you can control or fix your partner's drive. You are only responsible for your half here. I am saying that you can, by changing your attitude and actions, tip the tables slightly in your direction by having an understanding of where your partner may be in their own journey, where you personally are, and having a conversation based on finding a solution. Remember, SAME TEAM.

Sexuality/sex is natural and normal. From a basic 'we are animals' belief to sex is a spiritual expression and everything in between, sex is natural and normal. Honor your ability to feel pleasure and desire for connection. It is a beautiful part of the human experience.

Self-discovery is an integral part to having some authority over your sexual future. Answer these questions and come up with some of your own to see where you truly stand in your beliefs and boundaries surrounding sex? What is your sexual history? What beliefs do you have that came from your parents or your religious background? What are your limitations? What are your desires? What are your expectations? What are some myths that you have bought into (like men want sex all the time or women never want sex)? Get as clear as you can on your own answers to these and other questions about sex before you go trudging in to talk to your partner. Knowing what you want and don't want and <u>why</u> is essential in becoming responsible for yourself as a sexual being.

A fantastic book on this topic is Sex Without Stress by Jessa Zimmerman. Ultimately, your mindset or thoughts on sex will determine how you feel about sex. Sex is about pleasure and connection. Sex is the physical expression of this. There is no right or wrong way to have pleasure and connection with your partner as long as both of you are consenting.

When you talk to your partner in an open, honest way from a spirit of love, you will have a better chance at resolution than if you come with complaints and criticisms. Use I statements when sharing your desires for more, or less sex, for adventure or toned down interactions and for expressing your needs and wants.

A phrase that has worked wonders in our relationship overall, not just in the bedroom discussions, is this; I would love it if'. I would love it if you would do the dishes, I would love it if you would bathe the kids, and it can be applied in your sex life too. I would love it if…you would be more gentle, if you would be more aggressive. I would love it if you would kiss me more during sex or I would love it if you would check with me before pursuing the act of sex. Whatever it is that is true for you, speak your truth in love.

Here's the part no one likes. You don't get to choose how your partner responds. They may be receptive, they may not be. They may say no to your requests and you need to be ok with that. Your partner is an adult, with their own thoughts, wants, and desires. Respect their no. Just like you would want them to respect yours. It is only your responsibility to share your needs and desires with them, because they can't read your mind. It is not your responsibility or even within your capabilities to form their needs and desires. Accept that each of you has a different perspective. Come together to find an agreeable middle ground where both partners can find pleasure and connection.

Intimacy, pleasure and connection can come in many forms; it doesn't always have to be expressed sexually. Finding ways to connect with your partner outside of the act of sex can have a great impact on how sex is expressed. Developing pleasure and connection can be done through emotional conversations, doing something new together, shaking up your routines, nice notes, sweet text and small gestures of affection throughout the day. Focus on creating connection and receiving pleasure in new, and different ways. This will change throughout your relationship. I doubt we'll be sharing intimacy the same way when we are 80 as we are today. So become flexible, creative and open to new ideas on how to create connections.

 SIMON SAYS

Simon Says is a classic game with a simple concept; all you have to do is follow the commands and wait for the other player to 'screw up'. Just like those thoughts in your head, giving you 'commands' to live by and inevitably leaving you feeling like a screw-up. But who is this Simon? And what are these commands we are following?

Simon is all the shoulds and should nots that you tend to live by. Simon is the rules and expectations that you set for yourself and your partner. Simon is your, as Vishen Lakhiani of Mind Valley calls them, 'Brules', Bullshit Rules. We all have them and most of the time we are unaware that they even exist within us. They are all the beliefs handed down through the generations and in society, that we accept as normal and even as the standard for ourselves and others. It is a way for your brain to operate on autopilot.

The brain wants to operate at the least strenuous level that it can. It likes routine and consistency. The brain, your brain, doesn't really want to do things differently because that takes effort and energy and challenges the system. We like to think that we are 'thinking' everything through, but in reality, we operate more on an unconscious level.

How much thought are you really putting into your day? Ever drive somewhere and upon arriving think to yourself, I don't even remember driving here? Or do all your daily 'chores' without really thinking through the process of it all? When was the last time you really thought about how to shower or get dressed? So many of the beliefs and 'brules' we live by are unconscious and not really chosen by us.

Your beliefs, your Brules, your Simon may be society's commands or rules or your mother's voice in your head. Your Simon may be coming from religious doctrine. These beliefs come into the brain, virtually unchallenged as we go through life, as they are stemming from the subconscious mind.

I thought my partner was supposed to be able to make me happy, anticipate my needs (like I tried to do for him). I thought he should just know what I wanted, flowers and date nights, when to hug me and how to be there for me when I needed him. These are just some of the Brules I have struggled with....I continue to uncover more Brules and challenge them as time goes on.

Let's start with being aware of your Simons and challenging their instructions.

It all starts with a thought. I love this quote from Brooke Castillo; 'Problems are not problems until we think about them and make them problems.' It is your thoughts that create your feelings.

But can it be that simple? Put it to the test. When you have a thought about your life, yourself, your relationship with your partner, what is Simon saying? Do you hear things like, my partner should be making me happy? My partner should want to do nice things for me. My partner should just make plans, be a better parent, help out around the house, be able to organize, and shouldn't forget anything.

Maybe your Simon tells you all the things *you* should or shouldn't do. I should be the one who picks up the kids, cleans the house, takes care of vacation and date night plans. I should, I should, I should!!! Simon keeps you guessing and walking on eggshells and Simon is just waiting for you or your partner to screw up so he can buzz and make you feel like a loser.

How then can you turn Simon off?

Through awareness of your thoughts. Questioning your thoughts and beliefs and knowing your authentic self to see if these things line up with who you are and what you truly want. It is not a matter of 'lowering' your expectations, rather a questioning to know what is true for you. It's about having realistic expectations.

Begin by paying attention to the thoughts you have when you are feeling frustrated, angry, upset, disappointed... with your partner or yourself. Are you thinking things such as, I 'should' feel happy all the time? My partner 'should' compliment me more often? She 'should' enjoy cooking, he 'should' be more helpful around the house, she 'should' keep the children quiet, he 'should' spend more time with me and so on. Listen to your thoughts for a couple of days...really listen to them. Don't change them, just become aware of them. Once you hear the 'shoulds' your brain is telling you while on autopilot, you can now, from a conscious place, question those 'commands' from your Simon.

One of my favorite questions to ask my clients; IS IT TRUE? Is that thought or expectation true? Can that be proven in a court of law? Most of the time, our thoughts are just that, thoughts. They are not necessarily true. You are going to feel like they are true and your brain will want to resist any changes that you make in your thinking. Be patient. Show your brain who is boss.

Like Brules, your expectations may need to be adjusted. What are your expectations surrounding your relationship? Are you being realistic? Are you influenced by the love songs on the radio or those Disney princesses and heroes? Those types of things can lead to over romanticizing relationships and make life seem like a drama series on television.

There is an idea that prince charming is going to ride in on a white steed, rescue us from the dullness of life, and we'll ride off on the endless beaches and into the sunset. Instead, you get an average joe in a tinfoil hat with a styrofoam sword, swatting flies with it and asking when dinner is going to be ready.

Maybe you pictured being married to snow white or the beauty, instead, you got the beast. The idea that she will be loving and kind, the perfect mom and wife and a sexual goddess to boot, but instead she's stressed out, frantic and too exhausted to even think about having sex. Reality check!

Relationships aren't all rainbows, butterflies and romance. There are dark days filled with disappointment, anger, and loneliness. Boredom is real and perfect doesn't exist. It's not about lowering your expectations, it's about having realistic expectations of you, your partner and life. The perfect partner is not out there and you are not perfect either. It is when we come together, aware that we are imperfect people, that we can begin to complete one another.

Take some time to see what commands your Simon is saying. Ask yourself if these beliefs, thoughts and expectations are serving you and your relationship. Are your thoughts bringing you closer together or farther apart? Are your thoughts producing the results you want in your life?

Many times, your thoughts are coming from a place of defensiveness because you think that your partner is doing things or not doing things intentionally. As Dr Rusell Barkley says ADHD is an INTENTION deficit, not an attention deficit. If your thoughts and expectations need some refining, here's how you can do this.

Take control of your thoughts and give yourself a new, believable thought to replace it.

An example of how this can work;

THOUGHT-my husband should have noticed that the dishes needed to be done but, he left them there for me to take care of, does he think I'm his maid? CHANGES TO- I would love it if my husband would take care of the dishes. He probably didn't notice because his thoughts were elsewhere. I can certainly inquire if he would be willing to do them today.

Questioning your thoughts and replacing them with a more understanding, loving (and most likely) truer thought and then approaching your partner and using phrases such as, 'I would love it if'…you would do the dishes tonight before bed, will create a more peaceful, loving home for both you and your partner. Side note; specifying a time frame in which you would like something done will give your ADHD partner a deadline, which creates action and it also lets them know when you desire to have the task completed by. As an example, saying, 'I would love it if you would do the dishes before we sit down to watch tv at 8pm.' No guessing, no disappointment.

Ask yourself some hard questions about your thoughts. It can suck, but admitting that your thoughts are not always right, choosing to replace them with healthier, more productive and truer thoughts, will yield more peace in your relationship and life.

As Brooke Castillo teaches in the life coach school, your thoughts determine your feelings, your feelings determine your actions, your actions determine your results. Change your thoughts (to believable thoughts) and you change your results.

Don't mistake this for positive thinking. If that worked, there would be more millionaires and everyone would be happy. You've got to replace your thoughts with believable ones. Your partner isn't lazy, they may have task paralysis. They aren't ignoring you. They are most likely distracted. And on and on. Check your thoughts and see if there could be another perspective and form a new thought.

There are occasions in which you are projecting your thoughts or 'brules' onto your partner and making their actions mean something completely different than they intended.

Projecting is a coping mechanism rooted in shame, anxiety, and hurt. Ultimately, it's a defense mechanism. Projecting is typically when feelings can't be processed.

When my husband was quiet and introspective, I used to think that he was mad at me, and no longer loved me. I felt ignored, unloved, and scared. I would question his quietness, citing that his behavior towards me was rude and unkind and he should be nice to me and show me more affection, blah, blah, blah. In reality, it had nothing to do with me. He was just thinking, or as most men do, he was hanging out in his mental cave, minding his own business. Because of my own fears of feeling unimportant and unloved that stemmed from not feeling like I was good enough as a child, I was now projecting those feelings onto him. Apparently, I had some feelings from my childhood to process.

Projecting looks like:
- Being easily offended or triggered by others
- Blaming others
- Misunderstanding people's motives or position
- Emotionally checking out in order to get a better grasp on situations
- Out of control temper
- Reacting or judging people that remind you of those who you feel have wronged you

- Disliking a person because you see traits that you have within which you have not accepted.

Projecting is when you believe something about the world and then start to see it in others. Like looking through a lens that we have created by how we view the world and treating them as such, instead of seeing others for who they really are and seeing their actions for what they truly are.

The mind is a powerful place that shapes our reality. Be aware of where your beliefs are coming from and if they are indeed true or are you merely projecting them onto others.

Your Simon (thought) is most likely affecting you in your boundaries and your communication. Borrowing this from Brooke Castillo, your thoughts create your feelings, your feelings create your actions, and your actions create your results. Everything leads back to your thoughts. Let's explore ways to find what is true for you by defining your values.

BOUNDARIES

Finding your boundaries (or values) will make it easier to turn off your Simon by understanding what is truly important to you and your life with your partner.

The formal term to define boundaries is this; 'A value, characteristic or behavior that we <u>must have</u> in order to live our life, in any situation, as the person we wish to be.'

Ok, that's great, but can you break that down? Please? A value is a principle or standard, character is a feature or quality belonging to a person, place or thing, and a behavior is the action that is taken. So, to redefine a bit; A Boundary is a standard, a quality or an action that we must have in order to live our life, in any situation, as the person we desire to be.

We all have boundaries whether we are truly aware of and enforce them or not. You will know when a boundary has been crossed by the way your body responds to the 'offense'. You may feel angry, tense, sad, frustrated, helpless, lost, or a host of other emotions. Your body may present with a physical symptom; sick to your stomach, headache, muscle tension, and so on.

Setting your boundaries allows you and others to understand your expectations by making clear a set of morals or priorities that you have. And over time allows for adaptations or changes in how you want to interact with others.

When you live in a way that honors your boundaries, you are likely to have happy, healthy relationships. When you must constantly suppress parts of yourself and live below your boundaries, you will feel empty, unhappy, and unfulfilled.

Finding your boundaries does not mean that you become rigid and demanding or selfish, it's actually the opposite. Finding out what is truly important to you provides strength to be who you are, it means becoming more flexible and more caring. Well-defined boundaries allow you to put things in perspective and let go of petty issues. Boundaries are to keep you safe, not to control others.

Before you define what your boundaries are, it helps to know what areas to set them in. I believe for our purposes we can lump them into Physical and Emotional boundaries.

Physical boundaries include personal space, privacy, and your body. Violations include; standing too close, inappropriate touching, a tidy space, even looking through your personal files or your phone.

Emotional boundaries involve separating your feelings from others' feelings. Violations include; taking responsibility for another's feelings, letting another's feelings dictate your own, sacrificing your own needs to please another, blaming others for your problem(s), and accepting responsibility for theirs.

Until I studied boundaries, I had no idea that I was both crossing my partners and not setting healthy ones for myself. The area of emotional boundaries was my kryptonite. I did it all; took responsibility for his feelings, let his feelings dictate mine, completely disregarded myself to be pleasing to him (that was by my own doing, not his). I blamed him for all our relationship's problems too. But where did all this come from?

Our boundaries are shaped by:

- our heritage or culture
- the region we live in or come from
- whether we're introverted, extroverted, or somewhere in between
- our life experiences
- our family dynamics

A great place to begin is to identify your basic human rights. Judith Belmont, a mental health

author and licensed psychotherapist, offers the
following examples.

Basic rights

- I have a right to say no without feeling
  guilty.
- I have a right to be treated with respect.
- I have a right to make my needs as
  important as others.
- I have a right to be accepting of my mistakes
  and failures.
- I have a right not to meet others'
  unreasonable expectations of me.

Defining your Boundaries in 3 ways

1. Tune into your emotions.

Tuning into your emotions can help you to
better understand boundaries that you are
comfortable with and ones that you are not. You can
accomplish this by pausing and taking stock. How
am I feeling right now? What is my body trying to
tell me? What are the vibrations going through my
body? Where do I feel them? Describe it as if you
are describing it to an alien who isn't familiar with
emotions and how they show up. Something like...I
feel scared and it is a high frequency vibration that

95

feels like my body wants to shrink, become small. My muscles are tight and the contents of my stomach want to come out. I want to run. Or, on a more uplifting note; I feel excited. It is a high frequency vibration that makes my body want to dance and jump. I feel light in my body and there is a tingle in all of my muscles. My heart beat is faster and my eyes are bright.

Emotional discomfort is a sign that we need to attend to something. Pleasurable emotions let us know what/who we want more of.

2. Tune into your thoughts.

Do your thoughts about yourself become negative or positive? In what situations and around who? Tuning into how you think about yourself or how you are acting around certain people or in different situations can also help you to understand your boundaries. For example, if you are always anxious about spending time somewhere or with a particular person, that can be a clue that an important boundary is being crossed. Likewise, having happy and comfortable thoughts can be a sign that you are being respected and honoring yourself.

3. Get clear values.

Identify <u>what matters most</u>. Travel, time with loved ones, pay off debt, an education, a clean house, being active in your church or community. Different people will have different values and in a different order of importance.

Start by brainstorming all the things that are important to you. Don't worry about putting them in any kind of order just yet. Here are some ideas to get you started.

Financial Security; Compassion; Health/Fitness; Nature; Accomplishment; Creativity; Dependability; Loyalty; Beauty; Bravery; Gratitude; Love; Connection/Relationships; Learning; Leadership; Survival; Self-Preservation; Security; Adventure; Family; Work; Success; Calm; Freedom.....

Finding, setting, and maintaining healthy boundaries in any relationship can be complicated. Being in an ADHD affected relationship can be even harder because of the symptoms that are present with ADHD.

You may be holding it all together, and being responsible for nearly everything can lead to unhealthy boundaries. Assuming that you are the only person who can handle cleaning, cooking, child rearing, finances, and weekend plans is also a way that you are overstepping your boundaries. Are you following your partner around, making sure they pick up after themselves? Are making sure that they are using things the proper way (as we deem fit)? Are you touching your partner in ways that feel good to them or to you? Are you dominating your partner's time in order to feel important? Do you go through your partner's personal items, desk, phone, computer? Are you sacrificing your own needs to please your partner? Do you let your partner's feelings dictate your own? Are you communicating in a way to be heard or are you scolding and accusing in your tone?

Those are all ways in which you can be crossing boundaries, your own and your partner's.

Setting boundaries is more about discovering who YOU ARE as an individual and what is important and necessary for YOU to lead a happy, healthy life.

A boundary is a <u>must have</u> versus a wish. An example of a must have for you could be; mutual respect in a relationship versus obedience from your partner. Get clear on what is a must in life versus a want or desire or wish. Ask yourself if your boundary is for protecting yourself, or control of another. Learning how to set healthy boundaries by knowing what areas to set them in, how to honor both yours and your partners and putting them into perspective can lead to a happier, healthier relationship and certainly can result in more peace..

Remember, boundaries are to keep <u>you</u> safe. Your boundaries are your boundaries, meaning; you can set them but others are not obligated to follow your boundaries. They still get to choose their actions 100% of the time. Boundaries are for you to uphold, not to enforce upon others.

If you have this boundary; if your partner calls names during an argument, then you will walk away until they can speak to you in a more mature way, and your partner knows this is your boundary, they still get to choose if they call names or not. It is your choice to follow through on your boundary by stating that you have a boundary with this and walk away. or, you can stay and keep putting up with the name calling, thus allowing your boundary to be crossed..

When you are making and setting boundaries, make sure that you will follow through on them, otherwise they are just empty threats and you are just trying to manipulate and control the other person.

A boundary is, If you_____, then I_____ statement. It is not you telling a person how to behave. Using the format; If you name call, then I will walk away.

A boundary is not threatening a person that if they don't behave a certain way, then there will be a punishment. It's about you upholding your boundary.

As another example; If you don't like people who smoke and your friend smokes, you can absolutely let them know that you don't like smoke and prefer it if they don't smoke around you. Now, they can still choose to smoke around you. They get to choose their own actions. If you get mad, because you 'set a boundary' with them and they did it anyway, you are just trying to control them. They choose to smoke in your presence, then you can protect yourself by simply leaving the area where they are smoking. That is your right and how you protect your boundary. Do you see the difference?

Once you have defined your boundaries/found your values, both the ones you want respected and the ones you've crossed, you can then express them to your partner.

Owning your bullshit first and foremost is an important step. We are all human and showing your 'humanness' to your partner by owning up to the fact that you have an ugly, dark side and that you are aware or becoming aware of your own weaknesses and are committing to working on you can go a long way in healing hurts and resentments. You can do this simply by talking to your partner using I statements. Such as; I realize that I have some weak areas when it comes to boundaries (you can list a few) and I want you to know that I'm sorry and I will be working on these areas. Kind of a 'Please be patient while I am under construction' sign.

There is a right way and as you guessed it, a wrong way to express boundaries. In the middle of an argument is not the time, ladies and gents. In times of non-conflict, or at least not during a heated discussion, is best.

Your partner may feel threatened by your new found boundaries, and that is not what boundaries are about. Express that these are for your protection and health and that you understand that your partner gets to choose how they behave at all times. You are simply letting them know where you stand and what your actions will be in certain circumstances. That is all.

COMMUNICATION

Learning to communicate with your partner is so incredibly vital, and one affected by ADHD can increase communication issues tremendously.

Communication is where my partner and I have struggled the most. Both of us struggled to communicate with one another in a way that the other person could understand. We discovered that even one word in the sentence can have a completely different meaning to each of us and change how we interpret what the other is saying.

My favorite example of this, the word LOVE. After being together for several years, my now husband and I had a conversation about when we had first met and that within a few weeks after meeting he was telling me he loved me. I would smile and say thank you or I appreciate you, anything to avoid using the big L word. The word love encompassed so much to me. I had given it a meaning for myself that went something like this; If you love me, that means you are ready to commit to a long-term relationship, take on my boys as your own, move in with one another and begin making a life together. Turns out he gave it another meaning at that point in time. I love you, to him, meant that he cared about me, like he didn't want anything bad to happen to me, and was interested in spending more time together to see where things might go. He knew there was something special there, but that's about it. Nothing deeper than that. Boy, were we far apart on that one.

Realize that you each have attached meaning to words and actions that may or may not be true for the other person. You cannot, CANNOT over communicate.

Using a clarifying conversation has been most helpful for us. A clarifying conversation looks like this; I heard you say_____, I think you mean_____. Is that true?

Have a conversation based on learning what your partner is really trying to express. Become curious about the words used and the surrounding elements involved in the conversation. Get good at validating your partner. When you become curious and are striving to understand, a conversation that feels defensive and angry can become an opportunity for you to see that they could be frustrated, tired, hungry, embarrassed, or some other issue under all of that. It gives you an opportunity to stay on the same team and diffuse the situation. Being curious also helps to get you out of defense mode yourself so that you can approach the conversations with a solution focused mind and an open heart.

Learning about and validating your partner isn't to say, roll over and wet on yourself and take any verbal abuse. No...go back to setting a healthy boundary there. It is more about understanding your partner and letting them know you can see their point (not agree with it, but understand it).

Again, add ADHD into a conversation and you will find a few complications that may not arise in a neurotypical chat. Things like, your partner interrupting you, words that can be hurtful because they just said something without thinking it through. Conversations that wander all over the place. Discussions on the same topic over and over again. Monologues...from either side. Arguing just for argument's sake or complete withdrawal. And tons of defensiveness! I've seen each one of these communication issues as I reflect on my relationship. Remembering that your partner has a brain disorder when you are communicating with them tends to be a difficult thing to do, but remembering (at first this will take being vigilant) can help you to remain calm and frankly, gives you the control in the conversation when it inevitably starts to go south.

Let's look at some of the ways ADHD symptoms can affect the communication process and learn ways to overcome them.

Interrupting is because of lack of impulse, not because they want to talk over you or shut you up. It is hard for some people with ADHD to 'hold a thought' throughout a conversation. Or maybe your partner can only process one issue at a time.

- Try to read their body language and notice if they are getting antsy or distracted and pause to ask if they need to speak or share a thought.
- State the issue in as few sentences as possible and then ask for their input.
- Use a speaking 'tool'. The basic concept here is to have something that you hold when it is your turn to speak. One person speaks and then hands the 'wand' to the other. This in hand reminder helps to know when it is your/their turn.
- Set up stopping points.

Hurtful or rude partners. It's ok to point out, in a non-argumentative way, that their comment hurt you and ask if that is what they meant or if they would like to restate what they said. This gives them an opportunity to filter the words, because they didn't the first time, and choose a better way to communicate their thoughts.

In our relationship, we agreed that when something hurtful was blurted out that a simple 'OUCH' could be said to let the other know that what they said hurt you. That simple word gives the person who made a painful comment the opportunity to rectify it without having a major discussion on it by creating a PAUSE in the conversation.

The pause is not a natural thing for those with ADHD. Yes, it can be learned, but it will take time and effort on their part. By making small statements and allowing for a redo is your way to create a pause, when there isn't one.

Oh, the **wander conversations**! Lord, how many hours have been wasted on the wandering conversation? Too many to count here. You begin on a topic that you'd like to discuss, next thing you know you're talking about your partner's co-worker or the latest social media post they had just seen.

I'm sure you have had 4 hour conversations that could have taken 20 minutes if your partner could just focus. This leads to unfinished conversations or, at best, disjointed ones. This stems from distractibility.

There is so much input coming into our ADHD partners' senses. They can't, not because they don't want to, they *can't* filter the input. What you can do to help keep your conversations on track is to eliminate as many distractions as possible. Turn off the radio or tv, go to a room without much of a view or have your partner facing an area without too much to look at but you. Sometimes touching your partner's hand, arm or leg during a conversation will help them to stay present. Some ADHDers would do well with a stress ball or fidget item during a conversation. Providing an atmosphere with limited distractions and tools that help keep your partner focused can greatly reduce the length of time it takes to get through important conversations and be less frustrating for you.

'Peat and repeat' chats. How many times do you have to say the exact same thing to be heard? Yeah, well, part of ADHD dysfunction is memory issues. If you find yourselves discussing the same issues over and over again, get to the bottom of it by asking your ADHD partner if they do not remember, or are they just using that as an excuse? 9 times out of 10, they forgot. Your revisiting the issue may jog their memory, but until then, they really just forgot. So, if there is an important decision made, a schedule that needs to be kept or an agreement that they need to follow through on, for the love of all things holy…WRITE IT DOWN! Better yet, have the person with ADHD write it down and then put it in a place where they are going to see it. You may have to get used to sticky notes on your walls or doors, but if it helps to make life flow better for all, then enjoy your new decor. Some ADHDers have learned to rely on their electronic devices and calendars and those are perfect places for them to put this important info as well. In my experience, most will need another form of reminding that is more 'in their face' than the phone. Find what works for your person and home.

Black or white. I say black and you say white. As I am writing, I am reminded of my own words; 'it doesn't matter what I say, you always take the opposite side', 'It's like you just can't see my side' or 'you can't admit that I might be right'.

Oh, that chase for dopamine can be a bitch. Yes, they get a dopamine kick out of arguing. Arguing for argument's sake is one of the things the ADHD brain can enjoy for sure. Sometimes you can diffuse this, first,by being aware when it starts with your partner and then by asking a few questions.

Questions like; Is that what you truly believe? Is that your opinion? Do you feel that way? Where does that thought stem from? And so on. These questions, when stated in a way that is curious and not condemning, are to create a pause. It helps our partners to *stop* and think about what they are saying. Often when I have asked these types of questions, I get, I don't know, as the response. While that isn't an acceptable answer in my book, it does get him to pause and allows the opportunity for him to consider why he is arguing the point.

Knowing what it is that you are trying to accomplish with your conversation with your partner will help you to stay focused and to notice when it starts to go off track. On occasion, I will say, I really am not looking for an answer or argument with this subject, I simply would like to share my thoughts. Stay solution focused, stay curious to your partners' reasons why they are arguing and be aware when things are going astray and stay on topic.

Let's play **hide and seek**. You may also see the flip side of arguing for argument's sake, **<u>WITHDRAWAL</u>**.

Sometimes conflict can bring up too much emotion for the ADHDer and they will withdraw. The countless times I have said to my partner that he was like talking to a wall. No response, no emotion, blank stares and sometimes he would even fall asleep. Frustration 1000!

Withdrawal is a coping mechanism many ADHDers learned from a lifetime of rejection, disappointment, and bullying. Remember the emotional dysregulation? Yep, conflict has the same effect as does winning a prize. Emotions are extreme and way out of whack for what the actual situation is.

So many ADHDers have learned to stuff their emotions down in order to cope with the world around them. It is the emotional equivalent of walking away. While you are fuming from what appears to be a partner who is ignoring you, it is hard to calm yourself enough to address what is happening. Gather yourself as best you can, make a statement such as, 'I can see you are overwhelmed and I would like to discuss this with you, but would love it if you would be present while we are talking.' And If the conversation can wait, set up another time to have the conversation when you both can engage in it.

You have the right to be heard, but you cannot make your partner hear you, so being somewhat flexible here is key. The part here for you to remember is that you are in control of yourself, your thoughts, and your feelings and results.

Are you wanting to be heard or just vent? Are you looking for solutions or reasons to stay upset? Get honest with yourself. When you are solution focused and aware of your partner's emotions (boundaries) you can then set up the conversation or conflict areas in your life for success.

Addressing the elephant in the room with conversations....**DEFENSIVENESS**! Sometimes it seems like you don't even have to say 2 words and already your partner is defensive. Snarky comments and nasty tones, arms folded and angry facial expressions and you didn't even get a chance to say anything. What the what?! Anticipating criticism and fearing sensitive issues even before they hear what is being said stems from years of being told they were doing IT wrong or from having others tell them that they aren't reaching their potential or if they only tried harder- blah, blah, blah.

And...comorbidities can play into this as well. Like my partner with his O.D.D. (oppositional defiant disorder). Sometimes defensiveness is a way for the ADHDer to give themselves space, helping with their anxiety.

To bring down the wall of defensiveness with your partner, first be self-aware. How you are physically or emotionally reacting to the situation and your partner's reaction(s). Regulate your own emotions first. Use 'I' statements instead of 'you' statements. For example; I feel overwhelmed by the mess in the kitchen and would love it if you would help me clean it up. Instead of saying, 'you never help clean up the kitchen because you are lazy;. Shit, which one would you respond better to?

Sometimes just remembering the old saying 'treat others the way you want to be treated' will help you to remain calm, focused, and loving with your partner.

Try to not match the energy of a defensive partner. It can be easy to get into a competition of who is right, and who has a better solution or idea, but that can lead to lots of resentment. Learning to compromise is often best. I know it feels like you are always compromising. Please don't mistake compromising with always letting your partner be right or get their way. Hold boundaries here still. You both matter. You both have opinions and views.

The question is, can you come to a solution that both of you can live with? And if all else fails and defensiveness prevails...remember your boundaries. Boundaries are there to protect you. Simply state that this is a conversation that you would like to have and when your partner can entertain a conversation without defensiveness present that you are willing to continue and then, calmly, walk away.

Changing the words could/can to would/will. This simple change makes a huge difference in the way you communicate your needs and wants, not only with your partner but with your children, family, coworkers; essentially in all your relationships.

When you use the words could or can, they may come off as controlling or demanding. And those words can get interpreted by some as if you are asking if they have the ability to do something and are challenging them. Can you empty the trash?

Sure, I can. (That doesn't mean I will.) But if you say, Will you empty the trash? It communicates your needs clearly and requires a clear answer. Yes, I will or no I won't or even, yes, I will do it before bed. Change your could, to would and your can to will.

Keep your requests simple.
Some of us tend to over explain why we are asking for help or making a request to our partners. The K.I.S.S. (keep it simple, stupid) rule applies here. Be specific in your requests. I'm so stressed out, the kids are a pain and I haven't been able to get anything done today. Would you pick up milk on your way home today so that I can actually sit down for 2 freaking minutes? Becomes; would you pick up milk on your way home today? That is it! When you over explain, it sounds like a complaint and comes off as needy. Just ask for what you need from your partner and move on. They get to say yes or no to your requests, then you will know where you stand and what needs have to be met by you.

Stop playing the game of SIMON SAYS and start playing by your own rules. Confront your own set of 'Brules' in life. Take responsibility for your half of the communication errors and 'brules' you've put on your relationship. Question your thoughts. Choose what thoughts you want in order to feel how you want to feel. Set healthy boundaries and respect your partner's boundaries as well. Learn better ways to communicate your needs, wants, and desires.

Becoming self-aware, really knowing who you are, what you want and how to communicate with others will bring peace to your life.

 SURFS UP

Ride the wave of emotions!

A surfer waits and waits for the perfect wave and once spotted paddles like crazy towards it. Once the wave begins to crest, the surfer stands up, maintaining balance, and rides the wave in. They don't fight it or fix it, they just ride it in and feel the power of the ocean and the *peace* of trusting the wave. Much like the surfer, you can't control the wave, but you can learn to accept the wave you are on and trust the ride into shore with peace.

Notice it doesn't say ride the wave and feel the happiness, it says PEACE. Let's first look at the definitions of both happiness and peace.

Happiness is a FEELING of pleasure or contentment. Feelings are not sustainable. Sustainable means able to maintain at a certain rate or level. Something is sustainable if it can be maintained indefinitely. With that said, if happiness is a FEELING, can you maintain a feeling indefinitely? NO! Peace, on the other hand, is a quiet and calm STATE OF MIND or BEING. A state of mind or state of being is on a higher level of consciousness than feelings, and a state of being can be maintained indefinitely and is sustainable. That higher level of consciousness is an **intentional** thought process.

Feelings tend to run on automatic pilot. I like to refer to that process as our hamster brain. That cute little furry 'mind' critter just jumps on that wheel of emotion and runs like mad. Never really going anywhere, but man, it seems like it is. It believes that it's making progress. In reality, it's just going around and around, but staying in the same place. Our brains do the same thing when we do not consciously choose our state of mind/being. Once you master finding your peace, you will in turn feel happiness more often. A great side effect, don't you think?

Can I find peace even if my partner never changes? Yes, you can!!! How do you find peace then? The short answer is; first becoming *aware* and then *choosing* how you want to grow your inner self.

Now don't stop reading. This isn't some hocus pocus, far out spiritual guru, think positive bullshit. You cannot 'think positive' your way into a better relationship and peaceful life. That is crap that has been fed to you by well intended, but misguided people. Yes, having a positive outlook on things helps to guide thoughts in a good way, but it cannot bring about the growth and change needed.

As stated, becoming *aware* and then **choosing** how you want to grow your inner self is how you find peace. Awareness of self and choosing how you want to show up in your relationships with others and the world around you.

SHOWING UP

Choosing how you want to show up? What does that even mean? We are going to use the following definition of show up; *to be clearly seen; to come; arrive.*

You get to choose how you want to be seen, how you come to the relationship, how you arrive, which in turn will automatically change those relationships with your partner because you will present yourself differently and show up in your interactions with others in a way that you choose, not in a reactive way.

Yes, relationships will change, not always for the better. You may lose people and relationships along this journey and/or you may develop deeper, more meaningful relationships. But in the end, finding Peace is worth the wins and losses.

You have to change you for you. It's important to accept that you can't change your spouse. There will be no control on your part which way it goes. You can only control your contribution to the relationship and the other parties involved get to choose their contribution. At the end of the day, the goal here is peace within yourself. Changing your own behavior *may* trigger your spouse to want to make positive changes, but changing to manipulate your partner into changing will never work.

CONTROL AND CHAOS

Surfing is one of the most difficult and complex sports in the world. There are no 2 waves that are the same and the playing field is constantly changing. Winds, tides and swells are affecting the waves you surf, just like stress, sounds, sights, emotions, job demands, children and much more affect your partner's ADHD symptoms and how they present. The surfer cannot control the waves, and you are not in control of your partner and you certainly are not in control of the ADHD symptoms.

Relationships can be chaotic, unpredictable and feel out of control. When you take two people, their upbringings, beliefs, traumas, differences, and attachment styles, put them in a relationship and expect everything to go right, like some fairytale dream, you're going to be disappointed. Now add brain dysfunction to the mix. It tends to look more like the movie, *You, Me and Dupree*, where wedded bliss turns upside down when it becomes affected by a third party living in the house. The chaotic environment of a 'normal' relationship becomes 'enhanced' with ADHD living in the house.

I have never been accused of being a passive person, especially in my younger years, but dealing with 'Dupree' in our home turned me into more of a controlling monster than I ever dreamed I could be. Always uptight, making more rules and demands with each passing year. Suppressing my own desires and fun so as to 'model' what a responsible adult looks like. What in the actual hell was I doing? How did I get to that point?

Like me, you may not even realize that you are being controlling, or that it has gone to extremes in your home.

Being controlling or having controlling tendencies doesn't mean you are a bad person.

Controlling behavior is a product of anxiety and fear. It comes from a place of not feeling secure enough in yourself so you feel the need to exercise control over another person and/or your environment.

The fears that lead to controlling behavior are typically
- the fear of losing control
- the fear of the unknown
- the fear of failure
- and the fear of being at the mercy of another, which could stem from traumatic events that left you feeling vulnerable.

We become super controlling out of fear. Are you seeing how easily this may show up in an ADHD affected relationship?

CONTROLLING WAYS

Let's take a look at ways you may be trying to control. Writing your thoughts down on each of these areas can help you to step back and take an honest look at your controlling tendencies.

Are you...

- Calling all the shots?
- Making all the decisions?
- Do you tell your partner what they can eat?
- Telling them who they can be friends with?
- Crossing boundaries or privacy?
- Denying your partner space or alone time?
- Constantly checking in on your partner while they are away from you?
- Picking unnecessary fights out of nowhere? (because negative attention is better than no attention).
- Controlling spending? Dictating what, when, where, how money is spent, Or criticizing your partner's purchases?
- Have you begun isolating your partner, keeping them from friends or family in the name of protecting them or your relationship?
- Guilt tripping? This can take many forms but ultimately makes your partner feel guilty for having their own feelings and making their own choices.
- Complaining about all the things you handle and do for your partner and/or household?
- Using sex as a tool or putting unhealthy limits on what is ok in the bedroom?

- Gaslighting by making your partner question their own experience by denying or deflecting?
- Showing jealous behavior to hide your own insecurities?
- Using conditional love by either withholding until they do things your way or by doing nice things, expecting that now your partner owes you?
- Refusing to accept blame for your mistakes?
- Making degrading comments to and about your partner?
- Highly critical?
- Keeping a mental scorecard to whip out and use against your partner to get them to do things your way?

Do you....
- Need to be the center of attention?
- Move between complimenting and sulking, trying to get your way?
- Threaten behavior, threaten to leave?
- Use the I'm just joking statement after hurtful remarks or actions?

I know some of these may have struck a chord within you and you may have responded with anger or defensiveness. Or you found yourself

123

giving an excuse to justify your behavior. Perhaps you felt absolute conviction and brokenness. Either way, your response, your feelings here are ok. You are ok. Breathe. It's about becoming aware.

AWARENESS

Seeing yourself in ways that don't feel good is difficult. Remember, you are human. You weren't born knowing how to surf and you may have had a crappy teacher or no teacher at all. Just like you would show grace, patience and understanding to a child during their learning process and sometimes 'ugly' behavior; show yourself grace, patience and understanding during your learning process, through your ugly behavior.

You already know that you have a dark side. We all do. And like most people, you hide away anything that will show your bad side. But what if you embrace your bad? Here's what I mean.

Become aware of your 'bad' tendencies, attitudes, and behaviors. Notice them, study them. You may want to really analyze and notice where those came from (that right there may heal some old wounds and soften those 'bad' parts). Once you are aware of the 'bad' you can choose to heal things that may need healing and/or learn to accept those traits, those 'bad' parts of you.

Remember that acceptance doesn't mean approval. You can accept that you have controlling behaviors or tendencies and not approve or like it.

In being aware of your dark side, you then also have great power in choosing to let that run wild or to temper those tendencies. Awareness gives you the power to choose.

With a loving, kind spirit toward yourself, your true self, go through the list of controlling behaviors again and be honest...Do you see yourself in some of those? I know I did, in a lot of them.

Controlling behavior became my go to in all things. And even as controlling as I thought I was before I met my now husband, when I was confronted with the chaos of ADHD, my fears, insecurities, and anxiety went into overdrive, so did my controlling behaviors. Even the 'helping' was based on a need to feel in control.

Oftentimes, you think you will stop controlling when your partner finally shapes up and starts doing what you're telling them to do. The truth; you'll stop controlling when you realize it's your issue(s) and that it stems from insecurity, anxiety and fear.

The more you seek to control and do not get the results you want, the more it intensifies the fears, because the results (you think), are proof of the uncertain world you are living in and are so desperately trying to control.

Literally at the mercy of your partner's ADHD symptoms, like a ship being tossed around in a hurricane, your fear of complete destruction kicks in. This realization of being at the mercy of another leads to tons of anxiety and insecurity. It can create a lot of fear when old emotions surface and you don't want to deal with them. It is easier to blame, shame, or control your partner. But hiding from your root cause of controlling behavior is not going to cut it.

Diving into the ocean of feelings that have pushed you to the shore of controlling behaviors is unsettling at the least. But in order to change, you will need to swim around in there until you can find the under current pushing you in the wrong direction. Stop running away from your emotions and learn how to process them.

PROCESSING EMOTION

You may not truly know how to process emotions or even what the hell that means. Your emotions are indicators, like all those silly lights on the dashboard of your vehicle. They let us know how safe, stable, and secure we feel. Processing emotion or reading the indicators helps us to follow procedures to keep us safe, stable and secure.

One technique for processing emotion (taught by Brooke Castillo) that I have found helpful is talking to my alien....Ok, no...I haven't lost my mind. It helps to picture an entity that has no idea what emotions are. You could imagine you are talking to an animal, or do that.

Imagine telling a squirrel that you are sad, or depressed, stressed or excited, and happy. If you could get that squirrel to sit long enough to listen to you, it wouldn't understand what you are saying. Imagining that I am talking to an alien that has no idea what emotions are but willing to learn about them is easier for me.

In talking to this alien, it doesn't understand what happy means or depressed means...you have to explain what it <u>feels</u> like physically. Drop down into the physical body and ask yourself, 'where in my body am I experiencing this?' Notice and observe. Just ask yourself what's going on in your body.

I'll give an example;

I feel sad. Sadness feels like my shoulders are heavy, my eyes are droopy and can't look up. I don't have energy to move my body, everything feels weighed down. Or, I feel happy. Happiness feels like my body is light, my skin tingles, my heart beats faster.

Try putting other emotions in the physical by explaining what the sensations are in your body. You can literally think about an emotion and begin to feel that emotion in your body, even if that is not actually what you are feeling in this moment. Our thoughts are powerful!

By putting your emotions into a physical description, you can 'sit' with it. Just let it process in the body. Feel it physically. When you grasp this concept, you will understand there isn't an emotion that you cannot handle when you process it this way.

Emotions are energy in motion. It's true! When an emotion comes up within you, it creates a vibration through your body, which creates a physical response. Thus, the reason stress can create so many issues in the physical body.

A vibration won't kill you, it is simply a vibration. I'm not saying all the vibrations will feel good. Oh, no, no, no. But realizing it is a vibration bouncing around in there, creating physical and chemical reactions; helps to reduce the emotions down to a manageable process.

Instead of running from your emotions through controlling others or buffering and avoiding, you can learn to accept, feel and cope with your emotions. You become capable of relaxing into your emotions and riding that wave to the shore.

All emotions are useful and there for our benefit. Some emotions keep us from danger, some allow us to have compassion for others, some emotions give us connection. Our emotions are a gift.and not every emotion is going to feel good. Who told you that only positive emotions were acceptable and worth having, anyway?

Our emotions connect us to the world. You want to feel sadness at the loss of a loved one or anger over an injustice. You want to feel joy for others' success and pain for a defeat. You want emotions. You want to feel. It's not about not having emotions or stuffing them away, it is about allowing them, and letting them process without having to let them control you. Emotions are not the problem, the actions you take from a place of emotions can become a problem.

Once you practice awareness of your emotions and the vibrations they create in the body, you can accept them.

ACCEPTANCE

Now please pay attention to the word accept. Many take the word accept and make it mean approval. Those are not the same.

I can accept something or someone without approval being present. I accept that I can be a controlling person, but I don't condone or approve of the behavior I had or can still have.

Just like you can look at a toddler that is throwing a temper tantrum and not _approve_ of their behavior, you can _accept_ that they are tired, or frustrated and they really do not know another way to express themselves yet. Your acceptance of their behavior helps you to stay calm, show understanding and helps that child to process what is going on for them. In the same way; accepting your emotions, not condoning or approving of them and the behavior you are showing because of them; allows you to process them without judgment and self condemnation.

Acceptance is; 'ok, so this is where you are at and it's alright'. You don't have to live there forever, show yourself some love and understanding and give yourself that internal hug that says, 'it's going to be ok'. You don't have to act on or act out your emotions. You don't need to emote and you don't have to fight them and make them go away. You can feel the vibrations in the body and let them process.

Accepting your emotions and taking responsibility for them shows you that other's actions are almost 100% based on something within themselves and that it's not personal. It's not a personal attack.

Even though much of our ADHDers words and actions can be perceived as a personal attack or be taken personally by us, most likely it is our perception of them and their actions, viewed through our own personal lens that has us believing that it is personal.

IT'S NOT PERSONAL

Taking things personally comes from a negative self belief. Someone says or does something, which has nothing to do with you, until you have a thought about it and a core belief kicks in. Now you're triggered, and react because of your thought, not from what actually happened.

So many times, this happened in our relationship. I would say something to my partner, get no reaction or a grunt from him. I would think, wow, he really doesn't care what I have to say, I must not be important. Now my feelings are hurt, I'm angry. Cue the argument.

Truth was, he was distracted with a thought of his own or a 'thing' in front of him and really didn't hear me. He loves me, I am important and it really wasn't personal at all. Almost 100% of the time the other person has something going on that has nothing to do with you.

When you take your partner's actions or words personally, it can hurt you in two ways or at two different times; in the moment, and in later moments.

'In the moment' reactions, you can experience defensiveness, fight, flight, or freeze. 'Later on moments' can produce over thinking or ruminating and self torture, the 'ifs'. Both are unhealthy.

When you discover your core beliefs behind your reaction, you can learn to reframe what is going on both in the moment, and afterwards. Your partner's actions and words are coming from a place within them, from their own negative self beliefs. Remind yourself that things have less to do with you than you may think. It really isn't personal.

Typically, it is a negative self belief that keeps you in the 'its personal' mindset. We each have a way we view life that was formed by our prior experiences, environment, our personalities, society and culture. But your view may be distorted.

Much like a person who is aging and begins to hold a written word farther and farther from their eyes to be able to focus on it and read it, and one day someone gives them a pair of reader glasses and their whole view changes and they see the words differently. You may need to put on a pair of glasses and get a different view.

Two people can go to the same event and have a completely different experience. It is their view of the event that changes the experience for them. I can complain to my mother how my husband just sits for hours at night and doesn't help around the house and from her view she can see that he works a very physically demanding job and he is probably exhausted. My view is that I see how he is neglecting chores and my core belief makes that mean that he is neglecting me, or I'm not important. And holy shit, it actually has nothing to do with me at all and the man is just fucking tired.

We replay the event over and over in our minds, trying to change the end result, ruminating, overthinking . If they had only said or done this…if I had only said or done that… and so on. When we ruminate about something, trying to change the outcome we lose 100% of the time. You cannot change the past words or actions, you can only do it differently next time.

So what are the beliefs behind your view? Do you need some glasses or just to wipe the grime off the lenses you have?

List some times when you know you have overreacted or ruminated on a situation. Dive into what some of your reasons for taking it personally may be. Ask yourself why it is so upsetting? What did it mean for you?

Your brain is a powerful organ and if you tell it something and believe it to be true, it will spend all of its time collecting evidence for that belief. The good news is that you can tell your brain a new thought, a healthier thought that serves you better and your brain will gather evidence to support that belief.

Try on different views of the events that you reacted to and took personally. Try replacing the old thought with a new one and see if the feeling changes. Accept that the problem you are having may be due to your negative self beliefs and put them to the 'is it true' test.

You will find that most of your negative core beliefs are not true and are certainly not serving you but you can change these beliefs by giving yourself new believable thoughts.

As you learn to process these events post issue, you will increase your ability to do so in the moment. A few tips to help;

- First and foremost BREATHE! I know you've heard that before. Well, there is something to be said for just taking a deep breath when you feel triggered and repeating to yourself, 'this isn't about me' or 'I am safe'.
- Change your perspective by talking it out with a confidante, coach, or therapist.
- Get another person's view on the event. It can help you to see it differently.
- Step outside yourself, like watching a movie, play the scene over in your head, but replace yourself in the story with a stunt double.
- Check your boundaries. You may need to re-establish your boundaries.

Remember, just as you are viewing the world from your lens, so too is your partner. Just like the surf, it doesn't take the surfers skill level and abilities into consideration as it rolls to the shore; it simply moves based on its own circumstances at the moment.

There you are sitting on your surfboard; you've had some training on how to surf, you're feeling like a boss. You realize you can only control your choice of what wave to ride and how you move your body. You start paddling, you're excited and nervous, you pick your wave, stand up and begin to ride. The waters change, throw you to the ground and wash you ashore. Face down in the sand you get up, knowing that the water has no personal intention towards you and isn't out to get you, so you get back on the board and try again and again and again.....with the expectation that you will eventually succeed. You got this, hang loose!

WILLY WONKA

Ladies and gentlemen, boys and girls, the chocolate room....

"Hold your breath, make a wish.
Count to three, come with me and you'll be In a world of pure imagination.
Take a look and you'll see into your imagination.
We'll begin with a spin, traveling in the world of my creation.
What we'll see will defy explanation.
If you want to view paradise, simply look around and view it.
Anything you want to...do it!
Want to change the world? There's nothing to it.
There is no life I know to compare with pure imagination.
Living there, you'll be free if you truly wish to be."

I love this song from the movie Willy Wonka & the Chocolate Factory for this book. It is a reminder that you have the power within you, the power of creativity and imagination. You were born with it!

We as humans are amazing 'creatures'. And whatever your beliefs are as far as how you came to be, one thing is for sure, you were given a brain that can create. You can use your brain to create beautiful artwork, to create plans for a company, to solve so many issues in the world. You can use your brain to make an amazing dinner, or plan a fantastic vacation. You can also use your brain to create your own world…out of pure imagination. It really does come down to how you use your brain, you create your own reality.

You can use your power of creativity and imagination to create your life by interacting with the world and people around you in new and different ways. You can use your imagination to survive when times are rough. It's not about pretending that your current situation doesn't suck, because sometimes it's going to suck. Remember, in life ½ sucks, ½ is great. However, you can use your imagination to focus on the life you want, to inspire yourself to reach for better days. Athletes do this, wealthy people do this, leaders do this…and so can you.

The ability to imagine what could be, instead of what is, leads us to strive for the possible. It provides motivation, helps us set goals, and moves us from complacency, negativity, complaining, and blaming into a world of possibilities and hope. Grab your brain and tell it to 'come with me and you'll see a world of pure imagination.' You are the tour guide of your brain. You are Willy Wonka.

Understand that your thoughts are powerful and what you think about is what your brain will focus on. I'm not talking about some make believe life, or pretending not to see issues by burying your head in the sand, no. What I'm talking about is using your thoughts to create the life you want.

YOUR THOUGHTS

Try this…. Picture a rainy day. It's gray outside and cold. You think, well, this day is crap. The weather is yucky and I just want to sit on the couch and do nothing all day. You feel sad, depressed and have a general sense of unhappiness. Notice how your body feels this and where you feel it. Now, change the thoughts to it's raining and what a great opportunity to get some things done inside the house. This could be a great day to work on that special project I've been putting off. Or now I have the time to get that appointment made or call that person I've been meaning to call. You feel energized, upbeat, and happy that it's raining. Notice the change in your body. Do you see how changing your thoughts about the exact same circumstance can change how you feel? That is what I'm talking about when I say use your imagination to create the world you want.

I used to ruminate about my partner. I could barely entertain other thoughts and ideas because I was all consumed about him, his behavior, how I could right all the wrongs, how I could change him. Playing out every negative scenario over and over, trying to change the outcome. Preparing for future disasters. I used to wake up each day with a 'what fuckery awaits me today' attitude. I would create negative scenarios in my thoughts, and by the time he got home, I was so defensive and angry; ready to attack any little thing that didn't go perfectly. Correcting or questioning any word or behavior that didn't line up with how I WANTED it to be, or thought it SHOULD be. That is not conducive to finding peace, not for myself, not in my relationship or home.

Create a world in which you have all that you need. A world where you are fulfilled by you.

CHALLENGES

Yes, all relationships have challenges; and ADHD adds to those challenges. Sometimes significantly. But, you are miserable because you are looking outside yourself and your thoughts, and giving your power and energy away to another human being and to your circumstances.

There was a movie on addiction and in a scene where the girlfriend of an addict was talking to the wife of another addict. The girlfriend asks the wife, 'how do you do it? How do you deal with addiction?' The response was, 'I mind my own business.' The wife explains that instead of worrying about what her husband is doing, she focuses on herself, because there is a reason she chose this type of person. There is something within her that needs working on, too. HELLO! She minds HER business.

You can be mad, or you can understand that if you are causing your feelings with your thoughts, then you can change your feelings by changing your thoughts and that my dear, that is empowering!

LOOK INWARD

Stop looking towards your partner, career, children, parents, money, society and all the bullshit out there to make you happy. Fucking, make yourself happy! That doesn't mean get selfish and rude, it does mean create a world that fulfills you.

If you have lost yourself, take some time to remember that you are an individual. Some refer to this as self care, getting grounded, self-discovery, spiritual awakening or whatever the latest trendy phrase may be. What you call it matters less than what you do to find yourself again. Just begin right where you are. It starts with a decision. Decide to put yourself first. I know, that can feel so selfish to even say that, but, just like when you are on an airplane and they go through the spiel 'put on your own oxygen mask first' before you can help another, you MUST first help yourself.

I was so far gone (in my opinion) that I had to start with small steps. I spent an afternoon trying on everything in my closet. I put on each article of clothing and used two qualifiers for keeping or donating…do I feel comfortable and do I feel confident? If the piece of clothing didn't meet both of those, it got donated. It doesn't matter if you only have a few items left in your closet, let things go that don't follow the comfortable/confident rule. Over time, you can replenish your wardrobe. You can then carry this same thought process throughout your home, clean out cupboards in the kitchen, give away or throw away items you don't use anymore. Those products in the bathroom that bring you no joy or are outdated just collecting dust…get rid of them.

This only applies to your personal items. If they are jointly owned or owned by another person, please check with them before purging it. These are just some ways to clear the clutter and find yourself and joy again.

SELF CARE

If you have the time, scratch that, MAKE TIME to get out a loofah, exfoliate everything and soak in that tub for hours.

Self care isn't something you do once a week or once a month to recharge, it's something that can happen daily by doing small, easy things for yourself.

*Drink more water.

Don't underestimate the power of water. If you can tolerate it, drink water first thing in the morning as most people are slightly dehydrated then. Finding the right cup/bottle was a key thing for me. I call it my adult sippy cup, because that's exactly what it looks like. Bottled water would just sit on the counter all day. A glass wasn't easy to carry around. I found a particular bottle with a built-in straw worked for me...I've got 4. Find yourself a favorite container and drink more water.

*Practice gratitude.

When shit feels unbearable, you want to run away
or light it all on fire, look around and find a few
things to be grateful for. We all have blessings in
our lives if we just notice them and if all you can be
thankful for is that you didn't kill anyone or
yourself today, well, that's a start. Joking aside,
gratitude and misery cannot coexist. Appreciate
what you can and focus on that for a few minutes
each day.

*Get grounded.

The best way to do this, take off your shoes and
socks and go stand on the grass or dirt. Just stand
there and breathe and feel the connection of the
earth to your body. Now, it's not always possible to
do this so other ways to get grounded are to put
your hands in water, focus on the temperature and
how your hands feel, touch items near you focus on
the texture and weight of the object, savor food or
drink or scent, move your body and pay attention to
how your body feels with each movement, listen to
your surroundings-really listen, place your hand on
your chest and breathe, visualize a happy memory,
pet an animal, listen to music. Basically, get out of
your own head and pay attention to the physical
world around you; find something to focus on for a

cleaning. Wiggle your body. Remember when you were a kid? Skip everywhere you go today. Hopscotch your way to the car or washing machine. Yoga is amazing and you can find many easy routines for it online. Getting in motion helps to release those stored emotions as well. I found that free movement dancing can be an incredible emotional release and cleanses the spirit. Find what works for you.

*Meditate.

No, you don't have to sit cross-legged on the floor in some holistic center and repeat mantras and ohms. Take 5 minutes of quiet time, with no phone, no kids, no partner, nothing but your own thoughts each day, just breathing. Don't fight what thoughts come to you, don't try to 'only think positive', just be. Focus on your breathing. Breathe in for a count of 4, breathe out for a count of 7. The count is less the focus, just exhale longer than you inhale for.

*Sleep.

Get some damn sleep already! You've heard it before, so do it! Some people need 9 hours of sleep, some need 4. Find the amount that works for you and set it as a priority. There will be nights when it doesn't happen, it's going to be ok, no need to be strict about it. Just try again the next night. Listen to your body. Notice how you feel and if you need to head to bed earlier than 'normal', do it. Your brain needs to restore itself. Again, if it is hard for you to fall asleep, focus on your breathing and relaxing your body and mind.

*Grow a plant.

Yep, you read that right. Find an item you consume, like a tomato, get a tomato plant and learn how to grow it. Caring for a plant that rewards you with its fruit is therapeutic. I personally love to garden for this very reason. It doesn't have to be a food garden either, just gardening and watching the plants grow and attract nature to it is rewarding as well.

*Sit/stand up straight!

Oh, how many of you just heard your mother yelling at you? Ha, I did. Mom was on to something here. Try it, sit/stand up straight, right now. Notice how you feel when you do it. More confident, more centered, stronger. Having good posture helps you overall health, mentally and physically. And it's self care that can be done anytime and anywhere.

*Limit social media.

Come on y'all, you already know that shit can be toxic. Most people are posting how great their life is and you start comparing yourself and your life with their 'fairytale', social media life. What you fail to remember is that everyone has sucky days, and things that go wrong, but it's just not acceptable to put that on your social media. Limit your social media, stay off it for a week and see how it improves your mindset and peace.

*Phone a friend.

Yes, use that lifeline. Phone a friend, meet them for a meal or a drink. Take time to reconnect to the outside world. We can get so caught up in the ADHD chaos that we forget about family and friends. Don't text, call, see them in person. Set aside time for yourself to enjoy the important people in your life.

*Say no.

You read that right. Learn to say no. Stop overburdening yourself with events, people, the PTA, kid's sports, your partner's events, church groups, playdates and more. Your time is valuable, you are more important than a to do list and keeping up with the neighbors. Learn to say no to things that do not add to your life and are only sucking your energy out. And here's something else to go with it. You DON'T have to give a reason for saying no. Hahahaha. It's true. You can simply say no. No, I won't be there. No, I'm not donating to that cause. No, thank you. I'll see you next month. Whatever doesn't line up with you, your calendar, your needs or wants, just say no. Try it and you'll see how easy it becomes. Most people will just accept your answer and not even question it. If they ask for a reason, you can just say you have personal reasons. That usually quenches their thirst. If someone keeps pushing for more on that, they are just being rude and crossing a boundary. Really, who digs into personal reasons? Typically, no one does. Case closed, your 'no' is accepted.

*Take a moment

Add a quick face massage or special treatment into your daily bathroom routine. While slapping on that moisturizer, take an extra minute to give a simple massage.

*Read something that feeds your soul.

Keep a book in the bathroom or nearby where you eat, and read a few pages. Set a timer for 15 minutes and read some pages. Or listen to an audio book. It's a great option for many and can be done while accomplishing other tasks or while taking a walk. Kill two birds with one stone.

*Journal.

That feels like a big deal to me. I like to call it free writing. Jot thoughts down, write a poem. Vent on paper. Get the shit out of your head and out on paper. Burn it afterwards if you want, just write.

*Try something new.

Pick up a new craft, try a new sport, build something with your bare hands. It's exciting to challenge yourself and when you 'try on' new things, who knows, you may find that you really love it and now you've found something else to enjoy in life.

Give less Fucks!

Not everything deserves your time, your attention, your energy or concern. Pick your battles is another way to look at this. It's not about caring less, it's actually about caring more about the things that are truly important to you and letting others take care of, and care about the things that are important to them. Stop taking on other's cares. Learn what is important to you and give a fuck about those things.

GOLDEN TICKETS

Ticket 1. Check your thoughts about your partner. You can do all the self care, therapy, and self-improvement courses and still not find peace because your thoughts about your partner and relationship are still negative.

If you think your partner is incompetent, selfish, unreliable, and a defensive asshole; well, then no matter what you or they do, your brain will keep looking for evidence to prove your thoughts right. If you can learn to focus on the good traits (there was something that attracted you to them in the first place), then your brain will look for the evidence there as well.

Ticket 2. Remember the definition of Peace? Peace is a quiet, calm state of mind. That comes from a higher level of consciousness of INTENTIONAL thought process.

Ticket 3. In the moments when the world seems out of control and you're about to lose your shit….. Breathe. Inhale for a count of 4, exhale for a count of 7…repeat. Literally think, I am safe, I am ok. Recognize the emotions you are feeling, put a name to them if you can. Stop resisting the emotions. Simply breathe and let them vibrate through the physical body while remembering that no emotion can kill you, you are safe.

Ticket 4. Check in with yourself. Ask yourself what you need in this situation to find peace, to calm. And then listen. Be in touch with your own needs and learn to articulate them or better yet learn to give yourself what it is that you are needing in the moment of crazy frustration.

Ticket 5. Focus on the good. Gratitude for the life you have, for the issues you don't have, and little things you are thankful for. Focusing on joy is a great way to find peace in those 'what the fuck' moments.

FINDING PEACE

Finding peace, like many other practices, takes time. It is like a muscle that will gain strength with repeated use. This 'getting your thoughts to work for you, instead of against you', yeah, it's not easy, but it is possible. It will take a decision and effort on your behalf. You will fuck up and you will have to reset.

Peace can feel so foreign when you haven't experienced it for so long. And chaos can feel more 'normal'. Check in with yourself and see if you might be creating some of the chaos because you don't know what Peace feels like and it's scary. Peace may even feel boring to you and who really wants to be bored?

Remember, the brain wants to operate on autopilot, and it's easier to be set in a negative thought pattern or in a chaotic manner. Your primitive brain thinks it's protecting you or because chaos feels familiar. At first it may feel awkward, uncomfortable, and sometimes silly, but the more you do it the more it'll begin to feel familiar, preferred and normal.

Peace feels like being present; present in your life, and present within yourself.

Matthew Hussey, a British Life Coach, stated; "You are in a relationship with the person you are with today, Period!" and "it's safer to base relationship decisions on who your partner is today rather than on the fantasy of who they could

153

become." I will add to this…. Or holding them to who they were in the past.

Holding your partner to past mistakes, or behaviors, making them pay today for things they cannot change is unreasonable, unfair, and will only create more unhappiness and chaos.

Have the mind set when you wake up that today is all you have. Because it is! When those eyes pop open in the morning (first, practice gratitude that they opened at all) ask yourself, 'who do I want to be today?' or 'How do I want to show up in my relationships today?' This is incredibly empowering.

Getting out of regret and resentment over the past and letting go of worry over the future, you will be present in today. Today is the only thing you have control over anyway.

Much like the boat ride in the movie Willy Wonka; the journey into your own thoughts, patterns and behaviors can be terrifying and confusing, but in the end, the ride is worth it. It is worth finding that peace within yourself that you can sustain indefinitely.

 CONCLUSION

You CAN find Peace, it begins within!

Winning the game of connect 4.

Token 1- discover your unique relationship, your thoughts about your individual relationship and partner.
Token 2- educate yourself on ADHD and its symptoms and how they show up in your relationship.
Token 3- accept responsibility for yourself, your thoughts, feelings and actions and learn self awareness.
Token 4- learn what cycles you and your partner are in and work on your ½ of the cycle to stop them from continuing.
4 in a row wins!

The Song That Never Ends

*Become self aware
*notice what cycles you may be in and focus on changing your ½ of them

155

Shut Simon Down

*Become aware of your thoughts and the 'Brules' you're living by.

*Have **realistic** expectations for yourself and others.

*Set healthy boundaries and make sure you're respecting others boundaries as well.

*Communicate, communicate and communicate some more. Find communication skills, key phrases and techniques that work within your relationship.

Ride the Surf

*The more you change, the more your relationships will change. For better, or worse, so be prepared.

*Accept your partner and yourself for where you are in this moment and know that it is ok.

*You can only control yourself. Letting go of control can be scary, but trying to control will only move you farther away from the peace you desire.

Create your own 'PEACE' factory

*Take care of yourself and learn what that looks like to you.
*Learn to be aware of your thoughts and CHOOSE what you want to think and that will create the feelings that you have.
*Create the world you choose to create. You have the power to have PEACE in your life.
*Choose who you want to be today.

Imagine a life where you wake up each day with a sense of hope and a sense of humor. Enjoy each moment of the ride with your partner instead of hanging on for dear life. You can do that when you use these steps and find true peace within.

This is a process, one that may require help from a coach or therapist. You can reach out to us at www.thefluidmindcoach.com
email: thefluidmindcoach@gmail.com
or call 1-734-316-8711
We will do our very best to help you find the resources you need to FIND PEACE.

REFERENCES

Dr. Russell Barkley **30 Essential Ideas Every Parent Needs To Know**.
https://youtu.be/SCAGc-rklfo

Dr Amen **7 Types of ADHD**
https://www.amenclinics.com

Jessa Zimmerman Author of **Sex Without Stress**

Vishen Lakhiani founder of MindValley **"Brules"**
https://www.mindvalley.com

Brooke Catillo Master certified life coach and founder of **The Life Coach School**
https://thelifecoachschool.com

Matthew Hussey Life Coach
https://howtogettheguy.com

Melissa Orlov Author of **The ADHD Effect On Marriage**
https://www.adhdmarriage.com

Judith Belmont Psychotherapist and Author
https://belmontwellness.com

Gina Pera Author and Editor of **Is It You, Me or ADHD** and **Adult ADHD-Focused Couples Therapy**
https://adhdrollercoaster.org

Ari Tuckman Author of **ADHD After Dark**
http://tuckmanpsych.com/

ABOUT THE AUTHOR

Born and raised in a small Michigan community, K. Fritts has always had a love for helping others, and a passion for personal growth.

When she sustained a TBI (traumatic brain injury) in 2015, her battle with and for her brain, took her on a journey of education and discovery that led her to becoming a certified Life Coach in 2019 and a Transformational Life coach in 2020.

Her relationship and eventual marriage to a man with ADHD created a desire (or need) to study ADHD and relationships affected by ADHD symptoms. And in 2021 she earned her ADHD-focused couples therapy certification.

In her journey to find her own peace in what seemed to be a world of chaos, she has found techniques and practical tools that can be used by anyone to find more peace in their ADHD affected relationships and in everyday life.

Reach out at www.thefluidmindcoach.com